WHIFFLETREES
and
GOOBERS

WHIFFLETREES
and
GOOBERS

1,001 Fun and Fabulous Forgotten Words and Phrases

W. R. RUNYAN

Skyhorse Publishing

www.skyhorsepublishing.com

10   9   8   7   6   5   4   3   2   1

Library of Congress Cataloging-in-Publication Data
    Runyan, W. R.
    [Americana buff's word companion]
    Whiffletrees and goobers : 1,001 fun and fabulous forgotten words and phrases / W. R. Runyan.
            p.   cm.
    Includes bibliographical references.
    ISBN-13: 978-1-60239-131-4 (alk. paper)
    ISBN-10: 1-60239-131-9 (alk. paper)
    1. English language—Obsolete words—Dictionaries.   2. English language—Archaisms—Dictionaries.   3. Americanisms—Dictionaries.
    I. Title.

PE1667.R86   2007
422.03—dc22
                                                                2007016173

Printed in the United States of America

Contents

Introduction

In the early part of the twentieth century, while automobiles, trucks, and tractors were making their appearance, there were millions of horses and mules in the U.S. Most farming was done with horse/mule-power, and most goods was transported on horse-drawn vehicles. Considering the centuries involved in the development of all of those horse-powered contrivances, it is not surprising that a large vocabulary relating to horses and horse-powered equipment evolved. In particular, the names of the many parts of harness and wagons became a common part of conversation. The same thing also occurred for the parts of plows. In that case, though, it was not that there were so many parts of a given plow but rather that, over time, so many different styles of plows were developed that an extensive descriptive vocabulary was required. More complex implements such as binders and combines had many more parts than wagons, harness, or plows, but their individual names never became a common part of ordinary conversation. Along with the demise of horse-powered farming and transportation, when the recovery from the Great Depression of the 1930s began, other changes involving food and housing and home medical remedies also occurred in the United States. These changes in turn led to more changes in lifestyle and more unused or seldom used words.

As more roads were constructed, automobiles became more common, and as a result, by the 1920s there had been literally hundreds of automobile trade names introduced. Following that, there was a tremendous consolidation of the automobile industry and most of the names and the companies associated with them had disappeared by the 1940s. A handful of those vanished automobile names are included in the glossary, with the choice of entries being based on the childhood remembrances of various people and not on car sales or mechanical innovation. For example, the *Metz* is included only because my father once owned one and I spent weeks when a teenager trying to convert the remains of its engine into a lathe.

Many of the words listed can be found in a dictionary, but with meanings that may not be the same as those given here since these meanings are based on the usage of nearly a century ago. Some entries may appear to refer to more recent developments, but are in fact old terms still in use, although sometimes with a different meaning. While the initial intent was only to consider rural and small town words and terms no longer in common usage, for completeness, many terms that were mostly used in larger urban areas have also been included. As the list of words being considered for inclusion grew, it became apparent that many of those words were actually still in use, but were not particularly common. Further, in many cases their meanings were quite obscure. Since these words are still likely to be encountered while studying early twentieth century Americana and since it is often quite difficult to find their meaning, they have been included separately as an appendix. Note that if a word within the text of the glossary is printed in **bold face type**, then that word and its meaning will be found as a separate entry in the glossary. If it is printed in CAPITALS, an entry will be found in the appendix.

Most of the included terms are from sources contemporary with the first part of the twentieth century. However, there are also some words included that disappeared from common usage between the time of the Civil War and the beginning of the twentieth century, but which may still be encountered in old literature. The bibliography lists the books consulted when checking memories, verifying meanings, or searching for additional information or words.

The Words

A

AAA   Acronym for the Agricultural Adjustment Administration.

A-battery   See **B-battery** discussion.

Abdominal binders   See **Belly button bands**.

Acetylene generator   An apparatus, usually quite compact and only a few inches high, that consisted of separate compartments for water and calcium carbide and a means of allowing the water to slowly drip into the **Carbide** and produce acetylene. Such generators were a basic part of early bicycle lamps, miners' lamps, and other small portable acetylene lamps.

Acid phosphate   A constituent of **Phosphate** soft drinks. It was the source of phosphoric acid in the drink. There were a number of recipes for acid phosphate but they all contained phosphoric acid and various phosphates such as potassium phosphate and magnesium phosphate.

Acme harrow   A HARROW that used small wavy runners instead of teeth and was supposed to break up dirt clods more efficiently than other harrows.

Aermotor Company   First manufacturer of the "new" style of windmill, the Aermotor, in 1888. The design used was essentially that still in use at the beginning of the twenty-first century.

A-frame harrow   A HARROW with an A-shaped frame. It was pulled with the apex of the A to the front and, for ground with many obstructions, was very convenient to use since an A-shaped frame was much less likely to hang up on stumps or rocks than a rectangular frame.

Agate ware   Basically, the same as **Enameled ware** except that there would usually be a color and design to make the surface resemble agate.

Aggie   Not a student or graduate of an A&M (Agricultural and Mechanical) school but, rather, an agate marble.

Aladdin Lamp   Trade name for a coal oil lamp that had both a wick and a mantle and produced an exceptionally bright light.

Alemite   A method using pressure to inject grease into bearings. This method replaced the use of **Grease cups**.

Alligator wrench   The jaws were fixed so that the opening between them was V-shaped. The inside surfaces along the V  were serrated so that, in principle, any size nut could be slid along the V until the serrations on each side could grip it. In practice, the wrench really did not work and was generally quickly discarded.

Animal power A small treadmill intended for small animals like dogs and goats. Such treadmills were used to power small machines such as butter churns.

Antiphlogistine A medicated poultice dressing that was popular during the early part of the twentieth century. It contained glycerin, boric acid, salicylic acid, methyl salicylate, oil of peppermint, oil of eucalyptus, and kaolin.

Aqua fortis Nitric acid.

Artificial gas Before the development of an economical way of transporting natural gas, *artificial gas,* consisting primarily of hydrogen, methane, and carbon monoxide, was made near where it was to be used. There were several compositions of the artificial gas, depending on the manufacturing process used, and if there were enough hydrocarbons present to add color to the burning gas, the gas was referred to as *illuminating gas.* Usually coal was the starting material, but petroleum was sometimes cracked to give *Pintsch* gas.

Ash hopper A wooden container for holding wood ashes and allowing water to seep through them and leach out lye.

Auburn An automobile made by the Auburn Automobile Company of Auburn, Indiana. The company was started by the Eckhart brothers and sold to E. L. Cord in 1924. Production was from 1900 to 1937.

Audion The trade mark of radio vacuum tubes manufactured by the De Forest Radio Company. Audion was also often used even when referring to early radio vacuum tubes from other manufacturers.

early 1930s

3

Aultman, Miller & Co. An early farm implement manufacturer. They introduced the "Buckeye mower" (patented in 1859), which had two drive wheels and was probably the first successful hay MOWING MACHINE.

Autoharp A small zither-like musical instrument popular in the early twentieth century.

Axle grease Axle grease usually meant wagon axle grease. Its composition was variable but generally included tallow and either palm oil or linseed oil.

B

Babbitt or Babbitt metal A soft metal used as a bearing lining. It was usually a mixture of tin (50 parts), antimony (5 parts), and copper (1 part).

Babbitting The addition of the layer of Babbitt metal to the inside of a bearing.

Babcock milk tester Used to determine the amount of butterfat in a cream or milk sample.

Backboard A high sideboard on the side of a wagon. It was used to keep from over-shooting the wagon box when picking ears of corn and throwing them into the wagon.

Backstrap Part of harness. A leather strap attached near the top of a **Hame** and then running along the back of the horse and joining with some of the strapping that held the breeching in place.

Bailer   See **Well bucket**.

Baking powder can   Baking powder generally came in a thin, sheet iron can with a tight fitting slip-on lid. The empty cans were almost always saved for storage purposes and were particularly valued by children, who used them to store their treasures.

Bale   Usually a cotton or hay bale, which was cotton or hay compacted into a rectangular cross section bundle and held together by wire (baling wire for hay) or steel bands (for cotton). A cotton bale typically weighed about 500 pounds and a hay bale about 66 pounds. Hay is now typically compacted into round bales weighing up to a ton each.

Bale tie   See **Baling wire**.

Baler   See **Hay baler**.

Baling wire   The iron wire used to tie around hay bales to keep them from coming apart. In the horse-powered era, the wires were precut to length and came with a loop at one end. The wire was reasonably soft so that it could easily be slipped around the bale and tied. Cast-off wires from the bales became a mainstay for various farm repairs. With the advent of power balers, the wire was somewhat stiffer and supplied in rolls.

Balsam apple   Used colloquially to mean a **Horse apple**. Note that the dictionary definition of balsam apple is that it is the fruit of a tropical West Indies tree.

Bangboard   See **Backboard**.

Bark mill   A mill used to coarsely grind **Tanbark**.

Bark spud   A large chisel-like blade with a handle several feet long that was used to peel sections of tannin-rich bark from growing trees. (See also **Tan-bark**.)

Barley water   A nourishing drink made by boiling barley in water and adding sugar.

Barrel   For volumes of various size BARRELS, see the appendix entry.

Barrel hoop   Thin iron bands a little over an inch wide that were used to hold a wood barrel together. Such bands generally survived long after the barrel had disintegrated and were often cut into sections and used in various home repairs.

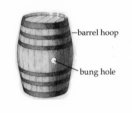
—barrel hoop
bung hole

Barrel planter   An early cotton planter design that used a barrel for the cottonseed container. The barrel had holes drilled around its midsection and was rolled along the ground so that the cottonseed could dribble out.

Bar-share plow   An early, crude turning plow with a wooden MOLDBOARD and flat metal bar for a **Landside**.

Basin former   An implement that ran along a **Lister** furrow and was usually pulled behind the lister. It had a rotating paddle that made little dirt dams every few feet to catch and hold any water runoff from rain or melting snow until it could seep into the ground. This method, a joint development of The Bureau of Agricultural Engineering and the Iowa Agricultural Experiment Station (R. B. Gray, "Tillage Machinery," pp. 329–346, Yearbook of Agriculture, 1938) was used in dryland farming, where any technique for conserving the available rainfall was of importance.

Battling bench   A wooden bench with a rough surfaced top that wet clothes were beaten against to clean them. The battling bench was sometimes used as an alternative to a **Rub board**.

Battling stick   The wooden paddle used to beat clothes when washing them on a battling bench.

B-battery   Before electric lines reached rural homes, anyone lucky enough to have a radio had to use a battery-powered one. Before the introduction of radios that operated on a six-volt car battery, a low voltage dry cell battery (**A-battery**) and a high voltage battery (**B-battery**) made up of a series of low voltage dry cells were required.

Beam   The beam is attached to the bottom of a **Walking turning plow**, extends to the front, and is terminated with a **Plow clevis**, to which an **Evener** or **Doubletree**

can be attached. The beam may be of either wood or steel, depending on when the plow was manufactured, or in some cases, on the intended kind of soil to be plowed. In the horse-drawn era, if the plow was likely to catch on rocks or stumps and there were enough horses pulling it to bend a steel beam, it was often preferable to have a breakable and more cheaply replaced wooden beam.

Bear grease A derisive term sometimes applied to excessive amounts of heavy grease used on someone else's hair.

Beegum See **Gum**.

Beer gallon 282 cubic inches. See also the discussion with the **Dry gallon** entry.

Beet plow A plow with a wide SHOVEL POINT that was used to plow up sugar beets.

Beet puller A plow designed to gently plow up sugar beets. There were two points, close together, that ran on each side of the beets and lifted them to the top of the ground.

Belly button band Generally made of a strip of flannel about five inches wide and two feet long that was kept wrapped around an infant's midsection until the umbilical cord came off, and was presumed to prevent an early hernia.

Bellyband A part of horse harness. (See also **Belly button band**.)

Belt dressing A wax-like material put on flat belts to prevent them from slipping.

Berry set A large dish for holding berries and a group of smaller matching bowls for holding individual berry servings.

Bifurcate harrow In the late 1700s, a name used for triangular (A-frame) HARROWS.

Binder An implement to cut grain stalks and tie them in bundles. **Row binders** were for crops such as corn that were planted in rows. **Small-grain binders** were for crops such as wheat that were not planted in widely separated rows.

Binder twine The twine used to tie binder bundles.

Bit See **bridle bit**.

Black alkali Alkaline soil caused by too much carbonate.

Black draught Black draught was a very strong laxative made from senna leaves and was used either as a powder, or as a liquid infusion of the leaves. The liquid infusion usually had some sort of flavoring added and was available as a syrup.

Black Sampson Echinacea.

Blacksmith One who works in iron and repairs iron implements.

Blacksmith coal Low-sulfur content coal that coked well and was used by blacksmiths. Very much sulfur in the coal would prevent iron from being welded.

Blacksmith tongs   A pliers-like tool with long handles that was used by blacksmiths to hold hot pieces of metal.

Blacksmith vise   A vise with a metal "leg" that extended downward and mounted against a bench leg. Such vises were much better than machinists' vises for holding large bars to be bent.

Blackstrap molasses   A term used by some when referring to plain **Molasses** and by others to describe molasses that had been overcooked and was extra dark. Blackstrap molasses now usually refers to the syrup remaining from the sugar-making operation after most of the sugar has been removed from sugar-cane juice.

Blinder   A leather cover on each side of a work-horse bridle to limit a horse's side vision. A workhorse bridle must differ from a riding bridle because of the peculiarity of horses' vision. Horses' eyes are remarkable in that they can see almost directly behind, as well as almost to the front. Further, they are particularly sensitive to

BLINDERS

movement near the edges of their field of view. This is very helpful to a cutting horse, but for a workhorse, not very desirable. Hence, most workhorse bridles had blinders attached to restrict the field of view and ensure that things to the side did not distract or "spook" the horse.

Blow torch   A small self-contained hand-held torch that burned some volatile liquid hydrocarbon such as gasoline. The fuel was fed to the burner by pressurizing the fuel tank with air from a small self-contained hand pump. The flame was not hot enough for welding and was mostly used to heat **Soldering irons** or pipe connections requiring soldering.

Blue norther   The cold north wind associated with a swiftly moving winter cold front. The name presumably came from the peculiar atmospheric color sometimes seen just ahead of the front.

Bluing   Bluing was a blue dye that was put in the rinse water in very dilute quantities before the days of bleach to counteract the yellowing of cotton goods generally observed after washing. A blue light of the proper intensity combines with yellow light to give a near white. (Note that this effect involves the mixing of light, not pigments.) The yellowing was mainly caused by the soaps that were available before the age of detergents when very harsh soaps were the standard.

Bobbed wire   Colloquial for barbed wire.

Boll   Cottonseed pod.

Bolster   Part of a wagon. It was a heavy wood beam just slightly shorter than the axle and was placed between the axle and the wagon box. There were two bolsters on a wagon. For more information, see the BOLSTER entry in the appendix. For a sketch showing the relative position of some parts of the wagon, see the **Hawn** entry.

Bolster plates   Two WROUGHT IRON wear plates, one attached to the front bolster, and one directly below it to the **Sand board**.

Bolster stake   A stake extending up from each end of a wagon bolster. The wagon box fitted between the two stakes.

Bonanza farm   From Webster's Imperial Dictionary, 1917: "A great modern farm, usually in the western sections of the United States or Canada, whose yields and profits are enormous."

Boomer   Colloquial for a load binder, a tool used to tighten chains holding down loads.

Bootjack   A metal V-shaped catch, attached either to the floor or to a wide board that could be stood on, and used to hook around a boot and hold it so one's foot could more easily be pulled out from the boot.

Boracic acid   Boric acid.

Bordeaux mixture   A fungicide for plant diseases that was made from cupric sulfate, calcium oxide, and water.

Boring machine   A drill press intended for boring into wood. Two cranks, one for each hand, usually powered such machines. Unlike the metal drilling post drill, which was usually in a fixed location, the boring machine was a self-contained machine that could easily be moved from timber to timber.

Bottom   See **Creek bottom** or **Plow bottom**.

Bottomland   See **Creek bottom**.

Box   A term sometimes used instead of **Hub boxing**.

Box supper   Similar to a **Pie supper** except that the box held two complete meals instead of a pie.

Bran tea   Made by boiling bran in water and then straining. Some recipes added honey and gum arabic. Said to be a useful remedy for hoarseness and sore throat.

Bread knife   A knife with a serrated blade that was used to slice bread.

Breadboard   A board ranging in size from about 15×20 inches to about 20×30 inches. It was usually stored like a drawer in the kitchen cabinet and was used as a small table on which to knead bread and roll out pie dough.

Breaker   A large, heavy plow for the initial breaking of prairie.

Breast drill   Like a hand drill except heavier and with a plate at the top that could be pressed against to increase pressure on the bit.

Breech strap   See **Breeching**.

Breeching   A heavy, laminated leather harness strap fitting around the horse's rump. It was fastened to other parts of the harness to keep the harness from slipping forward over the horse's head when the hames were connected to a neck yoke and the horse used to brake an implement.

Bridle   The headgear with which a horse is guided. It includes a **Bit**, which goes in the horse's mouth, and various straps that go around the horse's head and hold the bit in place. Horses become quite adroit at spitting out bridle bits so a well-designed bridle is a necessity. Unlike the rest of the har-  ness, which was quite late in development, bridles looking remarkably like those still used on horses first appeared in ninth century BC Mesopotamia relief carvings.

Bridle bit   A steel rod inserted in a horse's mouth and held in place by the rest of the bridle. Horses are guided by means of reins (lines) attached to each side of the bit. While oxen could be guided from a ring in their nose, horses apparently did not respond well to that approach, and almost as soon as evidence of domestic horses first  appeared in a region, the bit also appeared. Bits for riding bridles have always tended to be quite elaborate, but some of the basic workhorse bits looked just like those in the British Museum dating back almost a thousand years.

Broadcast   A form of small-grain planting in which the seed was scattered randomly and not in rows. Broadcasting was usually done by hand, with the seed being carried in a sack.

Broadcast seeder   An implement for planting small grain that was designed to approximate hand broadcasting. See **Endgate seeder**.

Brooder   After baby chickens were hatched, they needed some sort of shelter to keep them warm when sleeping. If there was an old hen available that would take them, it was common to put them with her, but if a hen was not available, or if too many chicks had been hatched, using a brooder was one solution. Brooder heating and temperature control was much like that of an **Incubator**.

Brooder house   A small building of only a few square feet that was used to house chickens right after they were hatched.

Brougham   A four-wheeled closed carriage drawn by one horse. The driver sat outside the closed cab. The original design was by Lord Brougham.

Brush harrow   A thick bunch of brush used as a HARROW. In one old article, the trimmings from pear trees are recommended.

Buck rake   A hay rake designed to travel along a hay windrow, collect a load of hay, and transport it to a hay stacker or **Baler**.

Buck saw   A predecessor of the bow saw. It had a wood rather than a metal frame.

Buckboard   A light wagon constructed by connecting the front and rear axles with a light framework of thin hickory slats so that a seat mounted on the slats was somewhat isolated from the bumps in the road. The buckboard is commonly associated with the wide-open spaces of the West, but an 1899 encyclopedia says that it "was born of necessity in the sparsely settled hilly regions of New England and the Middle States, when money was scarce and roads bad."

Bucket pump   A pump that used an endless chain with small buckets attached to it to pull up water from a well or cistern.

Buggy   A light four-wheeled conveyance intended for personal transportation. It was an American invention that was designed specifically to provide a fast, soft ride. The soft ride was accomplished by means of a light frame and ellipse-shaped springs mounted between the axles and the frame and oriented parallel with the axles. Buggies were generally pulled by one horse, had only one bench-like seat, and had a waterproof top that was usually made of leather. They were more comfortable for traveling than by horseback and were preferred by ladies, the elderly, and families with small children. Doctors, who often were called out in inclement weather, also favored them. Buggies did, however, have the disadvantage of requiring smoother ground to travel over than that required by a horse and rider.

Buggy pole   The tongue of a buggy. A tongue was used instead of shafts if two horses were to be used instead of one to pull the buggy.

Buggy wrench   A wrench used primarily for loosening or tightening the nuts that held the wheels on buggy axles.

Bull Durham sack   A small cotton sack that held Bull Durham tobacco. Empty sacks worked well for storing marbles.

Bull plow   An early, crude turning plow, introduced in New York State about 1810. It was similar to the **Bar-share plow**.

Bull rake   Another name for a **Buck (sweep)** rake.

Bull tongue   A CULTIVATOR plow point shaped somewhat like a tongue.

Bull tongue plow   A one-horse single-shovel plow using a bull tongue **Plow point** (**shovel**).

Bull wheel   A large, heavy, cleated wheel used to drive the mechanism of such implements as **Binders** and COMBINES.

Bundle wagon   In some regions, a **Header wagon** was used for hauling bundles dropped in the field by binders, and was sometimes referred to as a bundle wagon. Such a design was very convenient to use, since the high offside helped prevent the bundles from being pitched completely over the wagon while being loaded. In other regions, the wagons used for bundle hauling had a wide platform much like a hayrack instead of the flare-sided header wagon box, and the bundles were carefully stacked on it.

Bung   The stopper for a **Bunghole**.

Bung diameter   The maximum diameter of a conventionally shaped barrel.

Bunghole   The hole in the middle (not the top) of a barrel. (See the illustration with the **Barrel hoop** entry.)

Bushel   A measure of volume and usually considered 4 pecks (8 gallons). However, in the days when bushels and pecks were commonly used, U.S. dry measure, U.S. liquid measure, and

British Imperial liquid and dry measure were all likely to be encountered. As an example of how these different standards can affect calculations, consider the old saying "a pint is a pound the world around." At the beginning of the twenty-first century, if one weighed a pint of water from a kitchen measuring cup, it would be found to weigh quite close to one pound. Since a bushel contains 8 gallons, or 64 pints, then a bushel of water should weigh around 64 pounds, which is about what a cubic foot of water weighs. One would then conclude that the volume of a bushel is about one cubic foot. However, a bushel is really a dry measure and contains 2150.42 cubic inches (1.24 cubic feet). The "pint is a pound" assumes a liquid measure in which a pint is ⅛ of a wine, or U.S. liquid gallon, and contains 28.875 cubic inches, whereas a dry measure pint contains 33.6 cubic inches.

Bushel basket   A basket, generally made of very thin wooden slats about two inches wide that held one bushel. The quantity of many items of food for both humans and animals has been historically specified in bushels, but from a practical standpoint, only a few foods, even in the early 1900s, were actually packed in bushel quantities. Fruit was generally still packed and sold in bushel baskets, but things like a wagonload of corn were generally converted on the basis of weight to equivalent bushels for pricing.

Bush-head   A fruit tree injury thought to be caused by the **Tarnished-plant bug**.

Buster   A **Middlebuster**.

Bustle   A light framework (usually of wire) worn by women to puff out the back of their skirts.

Butt   A large cask, generally containing 126 gallons (two **Hogsheads**).

Butter bean   Lima bean.

Butter hand   See **Butter paddle**.

Butter mold   Before being sold to neighbors or stores, freshly churned butter was usually packed in wooden butter molds designed to hold one, or sometimes two pounds. After the butter had cooled enough to hold its shape, and before being sold, it was removed from the mold and wrapped in waxed paper. Some molds had a plunger to push out the butter after it became firm. Others had hinged sides that opened to allow the butter's removal.

Butter paddle   A wooden paddle for working (see **Butter worker**) and shaping blocks of butter. They were often used in pairs (one for each hand) and had grooves running the length of the paddle to facilitate the drainage of excess fluid from the butter.

Butter worker   When butter was taken from the churn, it still had appreciable buttermilk mixed in with it. The buttermilk was generally separated from the butter by hand kneading, but the butter worker was a hand-operated machine that made the task easier. The kneading itself was sometimes referred to as working the butter.

Butterine   Butter mixed with a little **Oleomargarine** to improve flavor.

Buttermilk Originally, the liquid remaining after butter churning, but since butter is no longer mostly made at home, buttermilk is usually bought, and is directly made by the addition of an appropriate bacteria to sweet milk.

Buttonhook A small diameter metal rod a few inches long with a handle on one end and a hook on the other end. The main use of the buttonhook was to help in  fastening shoe buttons. The rod with the hook on the end could be stuck through a buttonhole, hooked around the appropriate button, and used to pull the button through the hole.

Buzzard wing plow This plow was pulled by one horse, ran between the rows, and had a SWEEP that could be adjusted in width to match the row separation.

C

Cabriolet Originally, a two-wheeled, hooded, one-horse carriage, but also a four-wheeled, two-seated carriage with a very roomy back seat and a front seat intended to be used by a chauffeur. Later, shortened to "cab," the name was used for carriages for hire.

Cake salver A cake plate mounted on a pedestal.

Calcimine See **kalsomine**.

Calcium arsenate   A poison used as a dust to control cotton weevils.

Calf tongue   A narrow CULTIVATOR plow point sometimes used instead of the wider **Bull tongue**.

Calf weaner   Sometimes a calf is quite persistent and continues to nurse long after it should be weaned. Rather than keeping the calf and its mother in separate pastures, a calf weaner could be attached to the calf's nose. The weaner had sharp spikes sticking out from it that would cause the cow to kick the calf and keep it away.

Calk   Much like a cleat on a shoe, except that calks were for horseshoes. Calks were used to increase traction when there was snow or ice on the ground. In one design, the calks were an integral part of the shoe. In another design, each individual calk was driven into a mating hole in the shoe. In yet another, each calk had threads and was screwed into a threaded hole in the shoe.

Cambridge roller   One version of a **Surface packer**, so called because of its inventor, W. C. Cambridge.

Camphene   See **Camphine**.

Camphine   There seems to be some differing opinions on the meaning of this word. According to recent dictionaries, it is a mixture of turpentine and alcohol used in the mid-1800s in lamps. Because of volatility, the use of the mixture was soon abandoned. Thwing, in his book *Flickering Flames*, says the word is camphene, that it referred to turpentine only, and that the alcohol-turpentine mixture was called "burning fluid." Note that a Handbook of Chemistry lists camphene as the specific compound $C_{10}H_{16}$.

Camphor bush   See **Camphor weed**.

Camphor lamp   Probably a colloquial expression for a camphine burning lamp. See **Camphine**.

Camphor tree   See **Camphor weed**.

Camphor weed   The foliage of this plant smells strongly of camphor and was sometimes used instead of camphor. The plant *(pluchea camphorata)* belongs to the sunflower family *(asteraceae)*. Note: A 1918 wildflower book listed salt-marsh fleabane as *pluchea camphorata* and commented that the flowers had a faint odor of camphor. A more recent wildflower book that mentions the camphor weed refers to marsh fleabane as *pluchea purpurascens*. The *asteraceae* family is very large, and apparently changes continue to be made to the nomenclature.

Candling   Examining an object by holding it between the eye and a light source. See **Egg candler**.

Cane juice rollers   Rollers, usually turned by horses, that were used to squeeze juice from sweet sorghum cane stalks. The juice was then boiled down to make molasses.

Cane mill   See **Cane juice rollers**.

Carbide   Calcium carbide. When water drips on calcium carbide, acetylene gas is formed. The acetylene can then be used as fuel for lights.

Carbide lamp   A lamp designed to burn acetylene and to generate the gas from an internally contained supply of calcium carbide and water. Such light was usually brighter than that from coal oil-burning lamps and lanterns, and was often used for automobile, bicycle, and miners' lights.

Carbuncle   (1) A large, deep boil. (2) A red gemstone, generally a ruby or a garnet. However, Sherlock Holmes once had a case involving a blue carbuncle.

Carnival glass   Colored, pressed glass with an iridescent fired-on finish. It was introduced near the beginning of the twentieth century.

Carpet beater   Used to beat the dust out of rugs. They were used before the days of permanently-  fixed wall-to-wall carpeting, when rugs could be taken outside, hung over a clothesline or fence, and have the dirt beaten out of them.

Carriage house   A small, high-ceiling building for housing horse-drawn carriages such as buggies.

Carriage wrench   See **Buggy wrench**.

Case knife   A broad-bladed, rather dull, kitchen knife.

Casing   During the early years of the automobile, tires were sometimes called casings.

Casting   Another term for animal throwing. See also **Throw**.

Cat whisker   A fine piece of wire mounted so that it could be moved over the surface of the crystal used in a **Crystal detector** until a spot was found that would give good detection sensitivity.

Cat whisker radio   See **Crystal set**.

CCC   Civilian Conservation Corps. The Emergency Conservation Work Act of 1933 was the predecessor of the CCC, which dated from 1937.

Cellar   A small underground or partially underground room separate from other buildings. Affluent farms usually had cellars with masonry walls and concrete tops, but it was not unusual for the walls to be of loose rocks, and the top of logs covered with two feet or so of dirt. To minimize digging, the room was often not completely below the original dirt surface, but had the dirt that was removed from the hole heaped up around the part of the room above the original ground level. In cold climates, food was stored in the cellar to keep it from freezing in the winter. In warm climates, the cellar was used to provide a cool place for keeping food (e.g. milk and butter) during the summer. In tornado-prone regions, the primary function of a cellar was to provide protection from tornadoes.

Celluloid   One of the first synthetic plastics (1869), celluloid was made from cellulose nitrate and camphor. In the early part of the twentieth century, it was widely used for combs, hairbrush handles, harness decorations, washable collars, and toys, but because of its flammability has since been replaced by less flammable plastics.

Celluloid collar   A detachable shirt collar made of celluloid. Such a collar could be wiped clean with a damp rag and thus extend the time between shirt washings. The collar was held in place by being buttoned to the shirt.

Celluloid cuff   A detachable shirt cuff made of celluloid. Such cuffs could also be wiped clean with a damp rag and thus extend the time between shirt washings.

Centrifugal sower   Same as **Rotation sower**.

Chain drill   An attachment to be used with a carpenter's brace when drilling in metal. It allowed pressure to be exerted on the bit without having to press on the brace. This was done with the help of a chain running from the brace to around the work to be drilled.

Chaise   A light vehicle for personal transportation. Originally two-wheeled, and pulled by one horse.

Chalk   (1) A pale, thin, whitish ale. (2) Another name for **Chock** or **Choc** (see **Choc beer**).

Chamber pot   A pail with a capacity of about two gallons, and a tight-fitting lid. The pot was kept in the bedroom at night and used to minimize the necessity of going to the outhouse.

Chaw (of tobacco)   The amount of tobacco suitable for chewing at one time. Also see **Plug**.

Check-row planter   See **Corn planter**.

Check wire   The wire used to trip the planting mechanism of a **Check-row planter**. Such wire normally came in 80-**Rod** rolls.

Check wire button   Small bumps attached to **Check wire** every 30 to 40 inches. As each bump passed through the planter checkfork and tripped the seed valve, corn kernels were planted.

Cheese cutter   Cheese was usually delivered to the grocery store or meat market as a round block a little over a foot in diameter and several inches thick. The cheese was then sold to the customers as  small wedges cut from the big block by a cheese cutter. The cutter consisted of a turntable upon which the cheese block was placed, where a heavy blade pivoted so that, when pressed down, it made a cut from the center of the cheese block to the edge and thus cut off a wedge-shaped piece of the cheese. The wedge size was determined by how much the turntable was rotated between cuts. There were usually marks on the turntable to facilitate judging how many ounces a cut-off piece would weigh.

Chew-the-fat   In some geographical regions, chew-the-fat meant light conversation; in others, a lengthy and argumentative conversation.

26

Chicken plucker   During the depression of the 1930s, city dwellers would sometimes engage a "chicken plucker" who would, for a nickel or so, pull the feathers from a chicken to be dressed.

Chilblain   Sores that sometimes occur on hands, feet, and ears because of their prolonged exposure to cold (not so cold as to cause frostbite). Better-heated houses have minimized the incidence of chilblain.

Chimney   (1) The same as a flue. (2) See **Lamp chimney**.

Chitlins (chitlings, chitterlings)   Fried hog intestines.

Choc   See **Choc beer**.

Choc beer   There are several discussions of the origin and composition of choc beer (chock, chalk), but the one that seems most realistic is that the name was first applied to an alcoholic drink made by the Choctaw Indians from wild plants found in what is now Southeastern Oklahoma. However, by the mid-1930s, during the depression years, choc generally referred to any homemade, slightly alcoholic beverage. The drink was made from a variety of inexpensive raw materials, depending on availability, and was usually barely palatable. In the Southwest, the fermenting liquid that dripped from ensilage and collected in the bottom of silos was sometimes drunk. It was also not unusual for people to collect spoiled fruit from grocery stores, put the fruit in a bucket of water, and leave it under their house porch until it fermented.

Chock   See **Choc beer**.

Chock beer   See **Choc beer**.

Chopping block   A block of wood, usually just a short section of a log, used to lay small logs or poles across as they were being chopped into firewood. The chopping block provided support and kept the timber from flexing as it was hit by the ax. The block also kept the ax from hitting the ground and being dulled.

Cider-mill horse power   A stationary indoor horse power consisting of a heavy vertical shaft pivoted between the floor and the ceiling. The shaft had sweep arms attached to it near the floor and a large gear for transmitting power that was mounted high enough up the shaft for the horses to pass under it.

Cinnamon pie   A pastry made by making a ball of the scraps of dough left from making a pie crust, rolling it flat, then covering it first with a layer of butter or oleo and then with a layer of sugar and a sprinkling of cinnamon. The result was then either baked flat or else folded over in the manner of making a fried pie and then baked.

Circular harrow   A HARROW with a circular frame and constructed so that the frame rotated as it was pulled over the ground.

Circular slide rule   A slide rule comprised of two thin plastic disks and a cursor, all attached to each other coaxially in a manner that allows them to be rotated independently. The bottom disk is larger than the top one and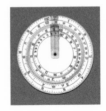

the various slide rule scales are printed near the peripheries of the two disks.

Cistern A deep hole dug in the ground, usually next to a house, and used to store rainwater that ran off the house roof. Cisterns were ordinarily used where no drinkable underground water could be found at a reasonable depth. The inside walls of a cistern were usually of masonry to prevent water loss from seepage and to prevent possible contaminated surface water from entering the cistern. Since the normal source of cistern water was rain, in periods of draught it was sometimes necessary to use a water wagon to haul in water.

Cleaver Regional name for **Hot** and **Cold sets**. More often, a butcher's implement.

Clevis Usually a U-shaped piece of iron or steel with holes at each end so that a pin could go through them. A clevis was used to connect two items, one with a ring at the end, and one that would fit in the U and had a hole in it for the pin to go  through. There were also a variety of special-purpose clevises like the cross-link clevis shown on the right of the illustration. See also **Plow clevis**.

Clinch nail See **Shoe last** discussion.

Clinker A vitreous material that collects on stove grates when coal is burned.

Clothes pin   A clamp used to hold clothes on a clothesline. In the early nineteen hundreds most of them were made by cutting a long slot in a wooden  dowel about a half-inch in diameter and few inches long. Later, most of them were small clamps made of two pieces of wood and a metal spring. That same design is still used in the twenty-first century, but generally with plastic rather than wood parts, for keeping plastic bags closed.

Clothes wringer   A pair of closely spaced rubber-faced rollers geared together, turned by hand, and used to squeeze the water from clothes after they were washed. A wringer replaced twisting the wet clothes by hand, and in turn was replaced by spin-drying.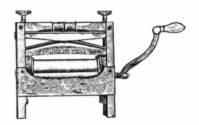

Coal hod   See **Coal scuttle**.

Coal oil   Coal oil (kerosene) is a light, nearly colorless liquid that is a major constituent of petroleum. It began replacing whale oil in the mid-1800s as a fuel for lamps and was used for that purpose until supplanted by electric lights. While electricity rapidly replaced gas and coal oil lighting in the cities, it was much slower in reaching the widely separated rural homes. The REA, originally put in place in 1935, then modified and extended in 1936, speeded the extension of power lines to rural areas, but it was well into the 1940s before the majority of the rural community had electricity and could switch from coal oil to electricity.

Coal oil lamp   A lamp designed specifically to burn coal oil. Also, see **Coal oil**.

Coal scuttle   A sheet metal bucket of about four-gallon capacity used for carrying coal from the coal pile to the stove. The scuttles had large lip-like spouts to make it easier to pour the coal into the stove without spilling any pieces on the floor.

Cock   (1) See **Haycock**. (2) A rooster.

Coffee pot   In the early nineteen hundreds, before the proliferation of coffee making machines, there was only one basic design of pots for brewing coffee. It differed from teapot design in that the pouring spout was at the top of the pot since, unlike tea leaves, coffee grounds tend to sink to the bottom of the pot.

Cold frame   An outdoor shelter for young plants that is covered with glass or, at night, with canvas. Its purpose was to help plants make a successful transition from a **Hotbed** or the house to an unprotected garden.

Cold set   A chisel with a handle on it and superficially looking like a **Hot set**. However, the edge is ground somewhat differently since the chisel is intended to be used on cold metal.

Collar   See **Horse collar**.

Collar hook   A hook attached to the ceiling or a wall and used to hold a **Horse collar**.

Collar pad   A cloth pad of perhaps three-fourths inch thickness that was often used under a **Horse collar** to provide extra protection to the horse's shoulders.

Colt   (1) While Colt is a longtime firearms manufacturer, the term Colt usually specifically meant a 45-caliber revolver. (2) A term still used for the young of horses or other horse-like animals.

Comport   A dish with a stem and a foot. Commonly used for holding fruit or jelly.

Comptometer   A desktop calculating machine used before World War II.

Conway buckle   A particular design of metal buckle used on harness to form a loop on one end of a leather strap. The Conway buckle was not intended to be regularly buckled and unbuckled, but instead was used to make a permanent connection. It was also sometimes referred to as a Conway loop.

Conway loop   (1) Same as a **Conway buckle**. (2) The loop formed in a leather strap when using a **Conway buckle**.

Cooling board A flat board on which a corpse was laid-out when the body was on view in the home. Such boards were mostly used in the South.

Cooper One who makes or repairs wooden barrels.

Cootie Colloquial for head louse.

Coppers Copperas (hydrated ferrous sulfate).

Cord (1) A measure of volume used primarily to measure the quantity of firewood. Legally, a cord is a stack 8 feet long by 4 feet high by 4 feet deep. However, a cord was often considered to be a stack 8 feet long, 4 feet high, and as deep as the length of the sticks of firewood, although that is a dictionary definition of a **Rick**. A **Cord-foot** is ⅛ cord or a stack 4 feet high, 4 feet long, and 1 foot deep. Often, even if the wood was not intended for sale, it would be initially stacked and measured as it was cut in order to judge when there was enough to last the winter. (2) A front-wheel drive automobile made from 1929–1937 by the Auburn Automobile Company of Auburn, Indiana.

Cord-foot 16 cubic feet. See also **Cord**.

Corn binder See **Row binder**.

Corn harvester See **Corn sled**.

Corn horse A light frame that could be moved about and was used to hold the first few bundles of cornstalks in place when making a **Shock**.

Corn husker   A metal hook that was strapped on to a hand to help in husking corn.

Corn knife   A knife with a blade about two feet long, used to cut down stalks of crops such as corn and cane.

Corn planter   In the early part of the twentieth century there were three distinct designs of corn planters in use. One was a one-horse implement primarily used for dropping corn kernels in a furrow, then covering them with dirt and pressing the dirt down; however, such  planters could also plant seeds of other crops such as beans, peas, grain sorghum and, with the proper attachment, cotton as well.

Another planter was the two-row two-horse check-row planter. While this planter was also primarily used for planting corn, other similarly sized seed could also be planted. It planted the seed in each row even with the seeds in the previous rows so that CULTIVATION could not only be up and down rows, but at right angles to them as well.

The seed spacing was done by stretching a long (up to a quarter-mile) length of wire with uniformly spaced bumps on it from one end of the row to the other. As the planter traveled along the wire, the bumps on the wire tripped the planter seed-dropping mechanism. The wire was moved over the planter's as each pair of rows was planted. As long as the new position of the starting bump was kept in line with previous starting positions, all of the seed locations along the entire row would be in line with the comparable locations on all previous rows.

The third planter was a hand planter that held less than a pint of seed corn, was carried by hand, and was used only where a small amount of planting was required, as when a poor stand occurred in a short section of a row, and some replanting was required.

Corn pone Cornbread made without milk or eggs, and usually shaped into small patties and fried.

Corn sled A horse-drawn sled with a cutting knife jutting out from one side. The sled could be used as an alternative to the earlier described **Corn knife**.

Corncrib A small building intended for storing ears of corn. The walls were of wooden slats separated from each other enough to allow good air circulation for drying the corn, but not enough for the ears to fall out of the crib.

Cotton blocking See **Cotton chopper** discussion.

Cotton chopper Cotton chopping, which is primarily the thinning of the cotton plants, is normally done by hand using a hoe, with the person handling the hoe referred to as a "cotton chopper." However, there have also been many attempts to build mechanical contrivances to thin the cotton, and those machines were also usually called "cotton choppers," but sometimes "cotton blockers." The term blocking presumably arose because, by chopping, the closely spaced row of cotton plants was cut into more widely spaced blocks of plants.

Cotton picker   (1) A person who picks cotton. (2) An implement designed to mechanically remove cotton fiber from its seedpod. It was developed before World War II, but did not seriously replace handpicking until after World War II.

Cotton sack   A canvas sack a few feet long that was pulled by a person picking cotton. The sack was used to contain the cotton as it was picked, and would hold sixty or seventy pounds.

Cotton scale   Regional name for a **Scale beam**. The typical scale was about three feet long and normally had a weighing capacity of 250 to 300 pounds. However, with a light counterbalance weight, these scales could be used to weigh only a few pounds (e.g., one or two chickens with their feet tied together). The same scale  design, although much larger and heavier, was also used at GINS for weighing baled cotton, which was usually about 500 pounds to the bale.

Cotton sled   One case when handpicking of cotton was not done occurred if an inopportune freeze from an early frost or late cotton planting caught a cotton patch full of unopened **Bolls** (seedpods). After the freeze, they would not open and the price offered by the GIN was greatly reduced. Thus, little labor to gather the bolls was warranted, but one quick and inexpensive way to salvage them was by dragging a sled, which had a V built into the front of it, along the row of stalks. The bolls were caught in the V, pulled off (stripped), and collected.

Cotton stripper   Rather than leaving the boll on the plant (see **Boll**) and picking the cotton fiber after the boll fully opened, cotton stripping pulls the bolls, both opened and unopened, from the cotton stalks. The cotton is then separated from the boll (seedpod) during the ginning operation (see **Gin**). The implement for doing the stripping is called a cotton stripper. Some were basically sleds (see **Cotton sled**), but others were wheeled contrivances that were the forerunners of cotton-picking machines.

Coulter   A flat steel disk about a foot in diameter attached, when needed, to the beam of a **Walking turning plow** to cut through grass and roots ahead of the PLOW-SHARE and MOLD-BOARD.

Country damage   An expression sometimes used to describe the damage occurring when cotton bales are not protected from the weather.

Coupling pole (reach)   The wooden beam, often an oak 2 × 4, that connected the front and rear wagon axles. It usually was long enough to stick out a bit past the end of wagon box, and was a favorite place for boys to stand. The reach of a buggy was really two pieces—more in the order of wagon **Hawns**, except longer and lighter. They connected the front of the buggy to each end of the rear axle.

Cowbell   A small bell hung around a cow's neck to help find the cow when it was in a timbered pasture.

Cowpoke   (1) A contrivance hung about a cow's neck to make it difficult for the cow to crawl through a fence. The poke was usually made of a light tree limb fork about three feet long. Factory-made models of iron straps were also available. (2) A colloquial expression for cowboy.

Cracklings   Fried pork skin or the crisp residue left after rendering lard from pork.

Cradle   A term sometimes used instead of **Cradle scythe**. The term also was used when referring only to the wooden frame attached to a scythe to convert it into a **Cradle scythe**.

Cradle scythe   A scythe with an attached light wooden frame parallel with and rising perhaps two feet above the blade. The **Cradle** purpose was to collect the grain stalks into bundles as they were cut, and thus make it easier and quicker to **Shock** the stalks. The concept of a cradle attached to a

Scythe blade

scythe dates back many centuries, and its versatility in small rough fields is demonstrated by the fact that it continued to be used in a small way in some parts of the US until World War II.

Craw   Part of a fowl's gullet.

Cream can   See **Milk can**.

Cream separator   In the early part of the twentieth century, generally a hand-powered machine for separating cream from whole milk, but sometimes a simple container with provisions for draining away the milk after the cream had risen to the top.

Creek bottom   The flat, low-lying land formed by deposits from a meandering stream. Such land is generally more productive than adjacent land and, before the widespread use of fertilizer, was much preferred for agricultural use.

Crib   A small building used for storing grain. See **Corncrib**.

Crop   (1) Another name for a fowl's **Craw** (2) A short riding whip (3) Any plant grown extensively for food or profit.

Crop duster   (1) A person who dusts crops, and usually referring to the pilot of a light airplane used in dusting. (The use of airplanes in the crop-dusting process dates back to the 1920s and was one of the earlier commercial applications of the airplane.) (2) An implement for blowing insecticide powder over a growing crop.

Crosscut saw   A large-toothed saw used for sawing down and cutting up trees. The two-man version was about five feet long, flexible, and a few inches wide. It had a handle on each end so that a person at each end could pull the saw back and forth. One-man saws were slightly shorter, wider and stiffer, and only had a handle at one end. There were, however, handles available for attaching to the other end that allowed two people to power the saw.

Cross-plow A second plowing, with the second plowing direction being different (usually at right angles) from that of the first plowing.

Crystal detector A detector of radio waves that consisted of a base and terminals, a piece of galena or silicon, and a **Cat whisker**.

Crystal set A simple radio receiver consisting of a **Crystal detector**, condenser, coil, and headphones.

Cupper (1) A name sometimes applied to a single **Cupping glass** with an integral rubber squeeze bulb for reducing pressure in the cup. See also **Cupping**. (2) One who does **Cupping**.

Cupping The process of pulling extra blood to the skin surface by placing a cup (cupping glass) in which the air pressure can be reduced, mouth down onto the skin surface. Cups with an integral rubber squeeze bulb for reducing pressure in the cup were available from the Sears catalog in the early 1900s. Historically, however, the reduced pressure was usually produced by heating the air in the cup before application and then allowing it to cool after the cup was pressed onto the skin. A man growing up on the East coast in the 1930s recalls that before the application of each cup to his father's chest or back (for fever reduction), a lighted wad of cotton dipped in alcohol would be stuck into the inverted cup for a few seconds.

Someone from West Texas remembers hearing about the cups being held inverted over the spout of a steaming **Teakettle**. A man growing up in East Texas said his mother would heat an empty soft drink bottle in boiling water, quickly wrap the bottle in a cooled towel, and then place the bottle, mouth down, on bothersome skin eruptions. In other parts of the world, animal horns with the tip end cut off were placed on the skin and pressure reduced by sucking on the tip. This is similar to a child's practice of briefly sucking on a hurt finger. Cupping was mentioned in English writing as early as 1519 and even in Greek medical treatises of Hippocrates' time.

Cupping glass A small glass of a few ounce capacity used for cupping.

Curry comb A comb used to comb dust and sweat from horses. It is comprised of several rows of metal teeth attached to a metal backing.

Cuspidor A receptacle for spit, usually from either snuff dipping or tobacco chewing. Generally considered the same as a **Spittoon**, although spittoons tended to be shorter than cuspidors.

Cylindrical slide rule A slide rule using a cylindrical configuration to allow several feet of rule to be included in an instrument only a few inches long. The one shown was made about 1900. It is twenty inches long and can give four-or-five place computational accuracy.

D

Damper   A means of controlling the flow of air into a stove. Usually, a damper was a plate that could be slid across air openings, but the damper in a stovepipe was a metal disk mounted inside the pipe that could be turned  from being parallel to the airflow to being perpendicular, completely cutting off air-flow. By controlling the air flow into the stove the size of the fire, and hence the stove temperature, could be controlled. Considerable skill in manipulating the dampers was required to control the temperature of a wood- or coal-burning cook stove during cake or pie baking.

Darn   A way of mending clothes, particularly socks. Instead of adding a patch, darning fills small holes or tears by using numerous interlacing stitches.

Darso   A hybrid grain sorghum. Its bitter taste discouraged birds from eating it in the fields.

Dash   A panel at the front of a buggy or surrey body to keep mud from splashing onto the occupants. Similar to an automobile dash.

Dasher churn   Instead of having a crank that rotated a paddle in the churn, the dasher churn used a wooden cross attached to a broomstick-like piece of wood that was moved up and down by hand to churn the cream.

Deere & Company   A farm implement company founded by John Deere to make steel MOLDBOARD plows. In 1868 it incorporated and took its current name, but Deere had been making such plows since 1837.

Depression glass   An after-the-fact term coined to describe inexpensive machine-made glassware produced during the Depression years of the 1930s.

DeSoto   An automobile made by the Chrysler Motors Corporation (Detroit, MI) from 1928–1960.

Dessert spoon   A spoon holding two teaspoons.

Dirt devil   See **Dust devil**.

Dirt drag   A framework of timbers, logs, or lengths of angle iron that was dragged over dirt roads or plowed fields to smooth them.

Dirt roller   A heavy set of rollers, each about three feet long and two feet in diameter, that were made of such things as sections of tree trunks, iron, concrete, or 2 × 4s bolted to old, heavy, CAST IRON wheels. Rollers were used for such things as crushing big clods of dirt and for pressing dirt down around freshly DRILLED seed.

Dishpan   A pan used for washing dishes. Usually the water would be heated in the pan.

Dope drink   A term that was sometimes used for the Coca-Cola drink because of what some people thought was included in its secret recipe.

Dort   An automobile made by the Dort Motor Company of Flint, MI from 1915 to 1924.

Double foot plow   Another (colloquial) name for a **Double shovel**.

Double shovel   A one-horse plow with two SHOVELS separated by about one foot. These plows were widely used in the South.

Doubletree   A two-horse **Evener**. It was three to four feet long, had a cross section of about 2 × 4 inches and usually was made of oak. In use, it had a **Singletree** attached to each end.

Doughboy   The name dates back to at least 1854, but in the U.S., it generally referred to an enlisted infantryman participating in World War I.

Draft   The force required to pull an implement while in operation.

Drag harrow   A name sometimes applied to A-FRAME or other spike-tooth HARROWS.

Drag saw   A saw that used a heavy blade much like that of a crosscut saw but, instead of being powered by a person at each end of the saw, it was driven by an engine. Such saws were sometimes called **Log saws**.

Draw (1) A small creek or gully. (2) The capability of the hot air escaping up a chimney from a stove to produce a draft and "draw" more air into the stove. (3) The difference between the outside circumference of the wooden wagon or buggy wheel and the inside circumference of iron tire to be placed on it.

Dress A term sometimes used to describe the work necessary to prepare an animal carcass for human consumption. It was most often applied to chickens, but was sometimes used when referring to hogs. It was not, for example, unusual for someone to look at a hog and say, "I think it will dress out at about XXX pounds," meaning that, after butchering, they expected the carcass to weigh about XXX pounds.

Dress form A light wire (usually) frame-shaped like a woman's torso that could be used to help properly match the different pieces of a dress as they were sewn together.

Drip gas A light gasoline-like hydrocarbon liquid sometimes occurring with natural gas. It collects in low spots in natural gas pipelines and can be drained out. In the 1930s, it was tapped by rural landowners and used in their automobiles.

Drum A **barrel**, usually one of steel.

Dry cupping Cupping done on undamaged skin. See **Cupping**.

Dry gallon   268.8 cubic inches. The units for dry measure and liquid measure were often somewhat different, and sometimes there was more than one measure for liquids. Examples were the differences between wine, beer, and water gallons.

Duesenberg   A very expensive car manufactured from 1920–1937 in Indianapolis, Indiana. The original company was founded by two Duesenberg brothers in 1913 to produce racing cars and marine engines.

Durant   One of the automobile brands made by William C. Durant's Durant Motors, Incorporated. It was manufactured from 1921–1932.

Duryea   The first successful gasoline-powered automobile built in the USA. It was built by Charles E. and Frank Duryea and demonstrated in 1893. By 1895, the brothers had established the Duryea Motor Wagon Company.

Dust cap   A head coverings made of cloth that looked and fitted much like a hairnet.

Dust devil   A small whirlwind that has picked up a substantial amount of dust. Dust devils are often seen in hot summer months moving across plowed fields.

Duster   (1) An implement for blowing insecticide powder over a growing crop. (2) Originally a long, lightweight coat worn to protect the rest of the clothes from dust and often worn when driving early open automobiles over dirt roads. Later, a woman's dress-length housecoat.

E

Ear trumpet A small bugle-shaped device intended to help those with hearing problems. The large end collected sound and funneled it to the small end, which was inserted in the ear.

Ebonite A hard material used for such things as combs that was made by heating a mixture of rubber and sulfur under a slight pressure.

Ecuelle An array of needle-like projections jutting up from a basin a few inches in diameter. The ecuelle was used for rasping raw, whole fruit and, in particular, to help in the extraction of oil from the peel of citrus fruit.

Edge creaser A small hand tool used to put a shallow decorative crease in leather.

Edging tool A small hand tool used to run along the edge of a piece of leather and slightly bevel it.

Egg candler A light shield that allowed only a spot of light about the size of an egg to shine out. Typically, such a shield was a metal chimney for a coal oil light. About half way up the chimney there was a hole approximately the size of an egg. By holding an egg in front of the hole (light source), it was possible to detect such things as embryos.

Eiderdown (1) The soft, fluffy feathers of the eider duck, sometimes used as filling for comforters. (2) A weave of cloth.

The 1895 Montgomery Ward Catalogue said their cloth resembled a sheep fleece closely sheared.

Eighth grade graduation   Before World War II, many rural children did not go to high school, but rather stopped school after the eighth grade. Consequently, in rural schools, an eighth grade graduation ceremony was common.

Enameled ware   Utensils made of thin sheet steel coated with a layer of a glass-like material were called enameled ware and were used when the utensils needed to be put on the stove or if the material being boiled was likely to discolor or react with metal of the utensil. When referring to such items, the "ware" was seldom mentioned, so that, for example, an enameled ware bucket became just an enamel bucket.

Endgate seeder   A planting method that closely approximated hand sowing. Seed was dropped onto a rotating disc and thrown off uniformly. The seeder was attached to the back of a wagon and powered from a rear wheel. The seed hopper was refilled as necessary from the wagon box. These machines were originally hand-operated (knapsack seeders), but by the 1870s had been attached to the back of a wagon.

Essex   An automobile produced by Hudson Motor Car company of Detroit, Michigan from 1918 to 1932.

Evener   A beam attached to a horse-drawn implement being pulled. Connected to the evener were individual **Singletrees** or **Doubletrees**. The purpose of the evener was to equalize the pull of each animal. By changing the pivot point, compensation for individual horse strengths was possible.

F

Fanning mill   A machine that used sieves and a fan to remove chaff from threshed grain. Fanning mills were originally built as stand-alone machines, but were later incorporated into threshing machines.

Fascinator   A lightweight scarf, usually knitted or crocheted out of lace, and used as a lady's headgear.

Felloe   Each segment of a ring of wood just inside the iron tire of a wagon wheel was called a felloe, fellow, or felly. Sometimes there were only two felloes per wheel, with each of them made of a long piece of wood bent into a semicircular shape. Other wheel designs used several shorter felloes per wheel, with each felloe being cut to shape rather than being bent.

felloe

Fellow   See **Felloe**.

Felly   See **Felloe**.

Fence pliers   Heavy pliers made especially for working on fences that used staples and wooden posts. Such pliers had the capability of cutting barbed wire, had heavy jaws flattened so they could be used to drive in staples that had worked partway out of the posts, and had pincer-like prongs on the side of the jaws so that staples driven into posts could be gripped and pulled out if the wire was to be removed from the posts.

Fencepoke   See **Cowpoke**.

Fender   A CULTIVATOR attachment used to keep small plants from being covered during early CULTIVATION.

Feterita   A variety of grain sorghum.

FFA   Acronym for **Future Farmers of America**.

Fid   A wooden pin, usually only a few inches long, tapered to a point and used to separate the strands of small rope. A marlinespike is generally much heavier, often of metal, and used on steel cable and larger rope.

Field cultivator   A two-wheeled CULTIVATOR used in seedbed preparation. They were an alternative to the HARROW and were also used to remove any weeds that may have sprung up between the time a field was harrowed and crops such as wheat were to be DRILLED or sowed.

Fiesta ware   Fiesta was the trademark of a pottery dinnerware made from the mid-1930s to the 1970s and favored by late-twentieth-century collectors.

Fifth wheel Before the advent of trucks, the fifth wheel was a semicircular iron ring attached to a wagon's front axle to give additional support to the rest of the **Running gear** as the axle pivoted during turns.

Five-abreast A five-horse **Evener** arranged so all five horses walked abreast. Also, five horses hitched in that configuration.

Five-horse string out A five-horse **Evener** arranged so that a pair of horses walked in front of two of the other three horses, which were side-by-side. Also, five horses hitched in that configuration.

Five-shovel cultivator A one-horse implement for plowing between crop rows.

Flags Common name for iris.

Flail A hand-threshing implement that consisted of two wooden sticks connected together by a flexible connection such as a piece of chain or a leather strap or thong. One of the sticks functioned as a handle while the other piece, the **Swipple**, was used to beat the grain loose from the stalks.

Flapjack When this glossary was prepared, "flap-jack" was synonymous with pancake, but there were many different formulations for pancakes and in the 1920s, households occasionally reserved the name flapjack for a pancake made from some particular recipe.

Flapper A name applied in the 1920s to young women who behaved in public in a somewhat risqué manner.

Flash bulb   A glass bulb containing a fine metal filament (usually magnesium) that could be ignited electrically to give a brief, intense flash of light for exposing photographic film.

Flash gun   A 1940 photographic textbook (Gilford G. Quarles, *Elementary Photography*, McGraw-Hill Book Company, 1940) describes the flash gun as a photoflash-lamp synchronizer for setting off **Flash lamps** simultaneously with the opening of the shutter. Later, when an electrical switch for triggering the **Flash bulb** was included in the camera itself, a flashgun was generally considered a **Flash lamp** made to be electrically connected directly to the camera.

Flash lamp   An assembly holding a **Flash bulb**, a light reflector, and a switch, battery and wiring necessary for igniting the flash bulb. The flash lamp had no provision for synchronizing the light flash with the camera shutter.

Flash light   The light from a small tray of flash light powder that was used before the introduction of flash bulbs to provide illumination for indoor photography. The light came from the burning of magnesium powder.

Flat   A box about a foot wide, two feet long and two inches deep filled with soil. Garden seeds were planted in it, and later the young plants were transplanted to the garden or a **Cold frame**. By the end of the twentieth century, a flat usually meant a shallow, flat box holding many small individual containers of plants.

Flatiron   A heatable hand-held iron tool with a smooth bottom surface that was used to smooth or press cloth. Unlike later irons heated by electric elements, flatirons were heated by setting on a stovetop. Also, see **Sadiron**.

Flour bin   A metal flour container built into some kitchen cabinets that was capable of holding about 50 pounds of flour. At the bottom of the bin was a **Flour sifter** through which the flour was withdrawn.

Flour sifter   A light sheet iron cylinder about six inches in diameter, open at the top, containing a hemispherical screen on the bottom, and a curved metal scraper that could be moved across the top side of the screen by turning a crank. While not listed in cookbooks as a prime reason for sifting, an important function of the sifter was to screen out weevils, which tended to be found in the flour after it had been stored for a time.

Flue stopper   A sheet metal plate used to close unused flue openings.

Fluter   A clothes iron in two pieces, with mating corrugated surfaces. The corrugations allowed dress ruffles to be ironed.

Fly net   A net made with cotton string or thin leather strips that fitted over a horse and helped keep flies away. The separation of the strings or strips had to be very wide in order to not cause the horses to overheat, but the motion of the netting kept the flies brushed off even though the net was far too coarse to directly keep out the flies.

Foot log   A log lying across a creek in such a position that it could be walked on to cross the creek without having to wade. Sometimes the log was merely a tree that had fortuitously fallen across the creek, but sometimes a tree growing by the bank was deliberately cut. In the summer, such logs were a favorite spot for sunning water moccasins, so it was wise to make sure the log was clear before starting across. Otherwise, one might find oneself trying to walk backwards on a small log.

Ford Model A   See **Model A**.

Ford Model T   See **Model T**.

Forge   A small, open furnace that burned coal and was supplied with forced air from a bellows or hand-operated blower. The forge was used by blacksmiths to heat iron enough (generally a red heat) to be shaped or welded. The left item in the  illustration is a blower. To the right is a forge. Air from the blower was piped to the bottom of the forge so it could flow up through the burning coal.

Four-abreast   A four-horse **Evener** arranged so all four horses walked abreast. Also, four horses hitched in that configuration.

Four-H club (also 4 H club)   Club work was "intended to help farm boys and girls become efficient farmers and home-makers as well as useful citizens and leaders." It was an activity that provided farm teenagers a certain amount of entertainment and socializing, as well as training for the life ahead. The four Hs stood for Head and clearer thinking, Heart and greater loyalty, Hands, and Health. Membership was for ages ten to twenty, and administration of the program was/is through county agents.

Four-horse string out   A four-horse arrangement such that one pair of side-by-side horses walked in front of the other two side-by-side horses. Also, four horses hitched in that configuration.

Fourteen-tooth harrow   A one-horse implement for plowing between crop rows.

Fowl rule   Devised by the Dept. of Agriculture and one of several formulas for estimating the volume of haystacks. First, measure the distance from the ground on one side of the stack, over the stack, and down to the ground on the other side. Multiply that number by the product of the stack width times the stack length and then by a factor, which varies from 0.25 to 0.37, depending on the specific stack shape, to get the volume of the stack in cubic feet. For other formulae, see the **Frye-Bruhn rule**, the **Outlaw rule**, and the **Quartermaster's** rule.

Franklin   An automobile that used an air-cooled engine and was made in Syracuse, NY from 1901–1934.

French harp   Another name for harmonica.

Fresno scraper   A dirt scraper with a single long handle for controlling dumping and the depth of dirt being scooped up.

Frock   By the mid-1900s, "frock" implied a woman's garment, usually a dress. However, in the early part of the twentieth century, a frock might also be an outer garment such as a short coat worn by a male laborer.

Froe   A steel blade a few inches long with a handle perpendicular to the blade. The froe was used for splitting thin sections from a log for use as shingles or planking.

Fruit jar   A glass jar used for canning food, regardless of what kind of food was actually canned. Fruit jars were mostly pint, quart, and half-gallon sized.

Fruit pricker   A fruit canning accessory that consisted of a base with several needle-like points sticking up from it (e.g. a board with sharpened nails driven through it) that was used to break the skin of fruit such as plums so that, if they were canned without peeling, the skin would not burst during the canning process.

Frye-Bruhn rule   One of several formulas for estimating the volume of haystacks. It was used chiefly in the Pacific Northwest. Measure the distance from the ground on one side of the stack to the top of the stack, over it, and down to the ground on the other side, and then subtract the stack width. Multiply that number by one-half the stack width times the full stack length to get the volume of the stack in cubic feet. This rule is reasonably accurate when the stack height is about the same as the width. For other formulae, see the **Fowl rule**, the **Outlaw rule**, and the **Quartermaster's** rule.

Future Farmers of America   The FFA was formed in 1928, primarily to promote vocational agricultural education in public schools, and was originally restricted to boys.

G

Gander   (1) Male goose. (2) A quick look.

Gang plow   A plow with more than one bottom.

Gauge wheel   A wheel attached to the beam of a walking turning plow to help control the depth of the furrow.

Gee   A verbal command sometimes used instead of reins to direct a horse to turn to the right.

Georgia stock   A one-horse plow primarily used for CULTIVATION. One identifying feature of a Georgia stock was the pronounced flare-out of the handles.

Giddap   Command to a horse to start or to move faster.

Giddyup   Colloquial for **Giddap**.

Gill   A unit of liquid volume. One gill equals one-quarter pint.

Girth   Part of harness. It is a leather band going around the animal's belly. Also, another name for a cinch, used to hold a saddle in place.

Goad   A light wooden pole used to prod working oxen to keep them moving.

Goathead   A seed of the puncturevine (*Tribulus terrestris L*). Such seeds have five burrs with 2–4 thorns each. The individual thorns are sharp and strong enough to puncture bicycle tires. Individual seeds always seem

Two or three times actual size.

to lie on the ground with the thorns pointed up, and such thorns are very painful when stepped on by a bare foot. The vine is found throughout most of the U.S. Occasionally, the seed of the field sandbur is also called a goathead.

Go-devil   Another name for a sled-lister-CULTIVATOR. The name go-devil was also sometimes applied locally to various other farm implements.

Goober   Regional name for peanut.

Gouber   Regional name for peanut. By the 1920s was being replaced by **Goober**.

Graham   Originally the Graham-Paige automobile. It was made from 1927 to 1941 by the Graham-Paige Motors Corporation of Detroit, Michigan.

Grain binder An implement for cutting small grain and tying the stalks into bundles.

Grandma A term often applied to the lowest gear on a farm truck when the truck had a four-speed transmission. The name presumably arose because the very slow speed of the truck was likened to that of a grandmother.

Granite ware Same as **Enameled ware**.

Grape hoe A plow that used a scraper instead of SHOVELS, and had a DISK to cut into the ground and prevent the scraper from causing the implement to slide sideways. In addition, one of the handles could change the disk direction and thus cause the implement to move laterally as it was pulled forward.

Grapple fork See **Hay grapple fork**.

Grass board A board attached to the end of a mowing machine CUTTER BAR, positioned so that it turned back the falling grass cut near the end of the bar and kept it separated from the uncut grass.

Grasshopper plow Another name for a **Rod** (sod cutting) **plow**.

Gravel In medicine, either small kidney stones or the disease that causes them.

Grease cup An assembly comprised of a small metal cup with internal threads that could be screwed down over a threaded base plate that was screwed into the housing of the mechanism to be greased (usually a bearing). The cup was packed with grease. When screwed down it forced the grease through a hole in the base plate and into the mechanism to be greased. Grease cups have largely been replaced by Zerk fittings and a grease gun that can force grease under pressure into the Zerk fitting and thence into the bearing. The means to inject grease under pressure using a gun and Zerk or comparable fitting was often called an **Alemite** system.

Great gross   Twelve gross.

Green corn stomp dance   See **Indian stomp dance**.

Grindstone   (1) A flat circular stone generally about two inches thick and twenty inches in diameter made of naturally occurring sandstone. It could be mounted in a frame and rotated to sharpen bladed tools such as axes and scythes. The sandstone used commercially was carefully chosen to have the right grit and a minimum of hard spots that would cause the stone to wear unevenly.
(2) Like the one just described and an axle mounted on a frame and fitted with a handle and/or a foot treadle to rotate the stone.

Groundnut   Usually a peanut (*arachis hypogaea*), which presumably originated in South America. Sometimes, however, it refers to the chufa (*cyperus esculentus*), a European sedge whose tubers are favored by hogs, or the bamberra groundnut (*voandzeia subterranea*), native to tropical Africa, or the hog peanut (earth pea).

Ground pea   Peanut.

Gully washer   A hard rain. In days before contour terracing, the runoff from a hard rain would generally wash small gullies in freshly plowed ground.

Gum   Colloquial expression for a beehive. The expression apparently came from an early practice of using sections of a hollow black gum log for a hive.

Gunnysack   Generally a burlap sack that originally held 100 pounds of feed.

Gyp water   Sometimes well water had so much dissolved calcium sulfate that it had an unpleasant taste and was called "gyp water," since gypsum is the common name for hydrated calcium sulfate.

H

Hack   (1) A horse kept for hire. (2) A carriage for hire. When automobiles began to be available for hire, the term "hack" was carried over to what is now called a taxi.

Hadacol   Hadacol was primarily a mixture of vitamins and minerals and was a very popular health tonic just after World

War II. Hadacol advertisements said it was good for such things as indigestion, loss of weight and malnutrition, nervousness and irritability, and some skin and eye disorders.

Hair receiver   A small covered bowl used for holding hair taken from combs and brushes.

Half sole   (1) See **Shoe last** discussion. (2) A wooden pole sometimes fastened to the bottom of a sled runner to protect it from the wear of sliding along the ground. The half sole could be much more easily replaced when it was worn than could the runner itself.

Hame   One of two pieces of curved tubular steel or iron-bound wood that fitted around a harness collar and to which a trace was attached. Sometimes, for decoration, the top of the hame terminated in a flattened brass ball about two inches in diameter.

Hame strap   A leather strap a few inches long and an inch or less wide, with a buckle on one end. It was used at the bottom of a pair of hames to connect them and hold them tightly around the horse collar.

Hand   The height of horses is sometimes given in hands, with one hand equaling four inches. Hand is an archaic English unit of length that has survived in this specific application.

Hand corn planter   See **Corn planter**.

Hansom cab   Designed by J. A. Hansom around 1834. It had a boxy body, two wheels, was pulled by one horse, and had provisions for the driver outside the cab. Often the driver stood on a platform at the back of the vehicle. The platform was mounted high enough on the vehicle for the driver to see over the top of the carriage.

Hard-water   Water that contains an appreciable amount of dissolved salts of calcium and magnesium. Such salts interfere with the action of soap. In the early days of the twentieth century, most rural water came from wells, and most of it was hard. Indeed, in some places, it was reputed to be so hard that a rock dropped into the well would bounce when it hit the water. Slight amounts of dissolved material in drinking water were often preferred because of the taste, but SOFT WATER was preferred for washing hair and clothes.

Hard water soap   Soap especially formulated for use in hard water.

Hardpan   A compacted layer of soil that is difficult for roots or water to penetrate. It often forms just below the depth of plowing, when plowing, year after year, is always to the same depth.

Harness   Mostly made of leather straps, a harness is used to connect draft animals like horses to loads to be pulled. The key to the success of the horse as an efficient pulling machine is in the design of a har-  ness that allows his strength to be transmitted to the load to be pulled without impairing breathing or blood circulation.

Harness buckles   Iron buckles at the ends of leather straps used on harness.

Harness hook   A hook attached to a barn wall and used to hold harness when not in use.

Harness horse   A bench with a pair of jaws for holding and clamping leather parts while they were being sewed together.

Harness Loop   See **Conway loop**.

Harness oil   Oil rubbed on the leather parts of harness to help preserve the leather and keep it pliable. One recipe for such oil was to melt, but not let boil, 3 pounds of beef tallow, and then add 1 pound of neat's foot oil and stir until cold.

Harness rings   Iron rings used to hold various harness parts together. Their diameters were usually between about three-quarter inch and 3 inches.

Harness snaps   Iron snaps used to connect various leather harness straps to harness rings.

Harness vise   See **Harness horse**.

Hart or harts   (1) A stag. (2) Often, specifically a five-year or older male red deer.

Hartshorn   At one time, shavings from a horn of a **Hart**. By the early twentieth century, spirits of hartshorn meant an aqueous solution of ammonia, and salt of hartshorn was an impure ammonium carbonate. By the late 1930s, "salt" had been dropped and hartshorn generally meant ammonium carbonate.

Harvester   (1) A reaper that used extra men riding on it to bind the bundles. (2) Any of various machines used to cut grain stalks in preparation of saving the grain.

Hat Pin   A metal pin used to hold a woman's hat in place on her head. The pin went from one side of the hat (in the vicinity of point A of the figure), through some of the hair near the front of the head, and stuck out of the hat on the  other side (point B) about ¼ inch. Depending on the style of hat being worn, the length of pin required might be from about three to eight-or-more inches. For the shorter pins, the pinhead might only be a spherical piece of celluloid ⅛ inch in diameter. The longer pins sometimes had ornate heads over an inch in diameter. Occasionally, a piece of fabric would be sewn over the pin head to make it somewhat match the hat.

Haw   A verbal command sometimes used instead of reins to direct a horse to turn to the left.

Hawns   Parts of wagon **Running gear**. They were wood braces used to keep the rear axle per- 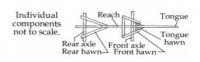 pendicular to the coupling pole (hind hawns) and the tongue perpendicular to the front axle (front hawns and tongue hawns).

Haworth & Sons   One of the first manufacturers of check-row corn planters. George Haworth began manufacturing them in 1853.

Hay bale   Hay compressed into a single block by a hay baler. Generally, in the early part of the twentieth century, the weight was adjusted so that there were thirty bales to the ton (i.e., each bale weighed approximately 67 pounds). Later, bales were made round and much heavier.

Hay baler   In the 1930s, a machine for pressing hay into compact rectangular bales. While some might be powered by an engine, most worked by using the power of a team of horses walking in a circle to ram hay into a horizontal rectangular guide until the desired weight was reached. These machines were stationary, so the hay had to be bought to them, usually on a **Sweep rake**. Later, the baler became mobile and followed the **Windrow**, picking up hay as it moved along. By the twenty-first century, hay bales were usually circular and might weigh as much as a ton.

Hay grapple fork   A set of large claw-like hooks used to pick up hay from a wagon or sweep rake and transport it up into a haymow.

Hay hook   A hand hook used when handling the old nominal 67-pound hay bales. Without a hook to grab the bales, handling them was awkward and required either holding the wires wrapped around the bale, or else wrapping ones arms around the bale. The newer round bales, which may weigh up to a ton, require a different approach.

Hay knife   A toothed knife about three feet long used to cut hay from a haystack. After hay had settled in a stack, it was

very hard to pull out chunks with a pitchfork. It was usually much easier and convenient to first cut off a section of hay with a hay knife.

Hay press See **Hay baler** for more details. The change in name from hay press to hay baler over the course of forty years illustrates how historians can sometimes be misled in assigning names. Early baling equipment was hand-powered and, in the 1898 Montgomery Ward catalog, a machine for making bales of hay was referred to as a hay press but, by 1929, at least one farm implement textbook was using both the terms "press" and "baler" in the same paragraph. By the mid-1930s, hay baling and baling wire were the common terms, with no mention, at least in the Southwest, of "presses."

Haystack dressing To minimize rainwater getting into a haystack, the stack was usually "dressed" by running a pitchfork down the sides of the stack and pulling out the stalks of grass near the surface that were crosswise, leaving only those that pointed out and downward. This procedure was very effective in producing an outer layer that shed water well. Unless a tarpaulin was used to cover the stack, the top of the stack was rounded off and dressed in the same manner. One of the key requirements in waterproofing was to keep the center of the stack tramped down more than the edges so that, as the hay settled, the center would settle less than the outside. The interior grass stems would then automatically tip down from the center to edge and force rain-water to run to the edge of the stack and down the outside.

Hay stacker A machine to lift a large load of hay from the ground to the top of a haystack. Horses usually powered stackers.

Haycock A small conical haystack, usually only three or four feet in diameter and six or so feet high. Such stacks were generally built to allow the hay to cure, after which it would be placed in larger stacks for storage. Things like peanut vines with the peanuts still attached might be stacked in cocks until the peanuts dried, after which the vines would be thrashed.

Haymow Usually barn attic space used for storing hay.

Hayrack A board frame with ladder-like ends about six feet high. The rack replaced the usual wagon box when hay was to be hauled. The frame was about twelve feet long and seven feet wide and, with careful stacking of the hay, would hold about as much as two horses could pull.

Headcheese Not cheese, but more like sausage. It is made by boiling a complete hog's head until the meat is cooked and starts to fall from the bones. The meat is then ground, seasoned, and chilled.

Header A grain harvester that cut the grain heads from stalks and transported the heads to a wagon.

Header barge See **Header wagon**.

Headerbinder A small-grain binder that was designed so that the horses walked behind the **Reel** and SICKLE BAR.

Header wagon A wagon used for collecting heads of grain as they were harvested by a **Header**. One side of the wagon box was higher than the other to keep the grain from overshooting the wagon box while being discharged from the header elevator.

Heaped bushel   The volume of a cylinder 18.5 inches in diameter and 8 inches deep, plus a cone of the same diameter and 6 inches high. This volume equals approximately 1.25 bushels.

Hektograph or **hectograph**   An appliance that could be used to make multiple copies from pages that had been written with special hektograph ink.

Henrietta cloth   A fine weave of cloth used in women's clothing. It was usually all wool, but sometimes had a silk or cotton warp.

Hercules-Club or **Hercules-War Club tree**   A small, thin-barked, thorny tree found primarily along the coast, from Texas to Southern Virginia, and sometimes confused with the Devil's Walkingstick. Colloquial names have included sting tongue tree, tickle tongue tree, PRICKLY ASH, and toothache tree. Slicing off some of the bark and chewing it or chewing tree twigs will make the tongue first tingle and then get numb, hence the reason for some of the common names.

Hillside plow   When plowing on a slope, unless one could go around and around the hill, part of the time the ground was being turned uphill, and part of the time, downhill. To minimize erosion, downhill turning over the whole field was much preferred. One approach was to build a plow with a MOLDBOARD and SHARE that could be flipped from one side of the beam to the other and thus turn the dirt to either the right or the left. Another solution was to have two complete plows, one right-handed and one left-handed, mounted on wheels and arranged so that either plow could be used. In the U.S., such hillside plows were called two-way plows because the plow could go either direction and still throw the dirt the same way. In England, they were called one-way plows because, regardless of the direction of travel, the dirt was only thrown one way.

Hinny   A cross between a male horse and a female donkey.

Hip strap or loin strap   One of several leather straps helping to keep harness **Breeching** in place.

Hitch   (1) The attaching of a team to the implement to be pulled. (2) The connecting linkage between the team and the implement.

Hobbler   (1) See **Kicker chain**. (2) A short chain with leather straps at each end that was used to fasten a horse's or mule's front legs close together so only short steps could be taken. Thus, hobbled animals could move about and forage at night but still not wander far away.

Hoecake   A bread made of cornmeal and water. According to a variety of dictionaries and cookbooks, the name hoecake orig-inated because in earlier days the bread was baked over an open fire on a hoe.  Considering what a hoe looks like now (pg 70), such an explanation hardly seems reasonable, but in colonial days, some 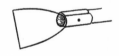 hoes looked like the one shown on the right below and the explanation does seem reasonable.

Hog plow   An early, crude turning plow, supplanted by the **Bull plow**.

Hog scraper   One of the early steps in hog butchering was to immerse the carcass for a few minutes in boiling water to loosen the hair. The hair was then scraped off with a *hog scraper*, which consisted of a short, round, wooden handle with a cup-shaped steel disk at one or both ends.

Hogback   A sharp ridge running along the top of a hill.

Hogging down   A term sometimes used to describe the practice of allowing hogs to eat a crop such as corn directly from the stalks rather than being fed harvested grain. The amount eaten each day could be neither measured nor controlled, but it was observed that eating was not excessive.

Hogshead   (1) A unit of liquid capacity equal to two 31.5 gallon barrels. (2) A large barrel of 63-gallon capacity.

Holler   Colloquial for **Hollow**.

Hollow   Small valley.

Hoop knife   A kind of drawknife used by **Coopers** in the making of barrels.

Hoop snake   A hoop snake could take its tail in its mouth, form itself into a hoop, and roll along the ground at tremendous

speed. Hoop snakes rolling along
were to be absolutely avoided since
they could easily outrun a boy and
had a deadly stinger on the end of
their tail that was dart-like and
could be shot out for a considerable distance. The stinger was
actually nonpoisonous, nondetachable, and of a horn-like
material about ⅛ inch long. In truth, of course, the whole
behavior was the figment of someone's active imagination.
Raymond L. Ditmar's 1939 *North American Snakes* suggested
that the origin of the myth lay in the fact that instead of
coiling, this particular snake sometimes formed itself into a
circle when resting.

Hoover cart   For very small farms with only one horse or
mule, a two-wheeled cart was often used instead of a light one-
horse wagon because carts were much cheaper. In some sections of the country during the Depression years of the 1930s,
homemade carts were referred to as Hoover carts in "honor"
of President Hoover, who was widely believed to have caused
the depression.

Hopperdozer   The hopperdozer consisted of a high-backed
sheet iron tray on sled runners and was dragged through grass
or weeds containing grasshoppers. As the grasshoppers jumped
up and hit the high back, they would fall down into the tray and
be killed by a thin layer of kerosene floating on water in the
bottom of the tray.

Horse apple   Fruit of the Osage orange (*bois d'arc*) tree.

Horse brass   A round brass medallion about three inches in diameter attached to horse harness for decoration. Used more generally in Europe than in the USA.

Horse collar   A band of leather or cloth, stuffed with straw or sawdust, that fits around a horse's or mule's neck, rests against the animal's shoulders, and presents a broad, firm, load-bearing surface to the shoulders.

Horse hoe   An early name for a CULTIVATOR, particularly in England.

Horse liniment   Generally, a derisive term applied to any strong and disagreeable liniment.

Horse nail   See **Horseshoe nail**.

Horse power   A machine that allows walking horses to power rotating machinery. One, two, three, or more equally spaced sweep arms several feet long to which horses were hitched radiated from a hub. Ahead of each sweep was an additional light arm (lead pole) to which the horses' bridles were attached in order to constrain the horses to walk in a circular path. The horses pulled the sweep(s) around and caused the hub to rotate. The hub was connected by gears to a drive shaft (**Tumbling rod**) which ran close enough to the ground for the horses to step over it each time they came around. Once outside the horses' path, the shaft could either be directly coupled or belted to the machine to be powered. Most horse powers were portable and mounted on either skids or wheels, but fixed installations were sometimes built inside barns.

Horse road   A term used near the end of the nineteenth century for public conveyances running on a track and using horses to move the car(s).

Horseshoe calk   See **Calk**.

Horseshoe nail ring   While of not much practical use other than to nail horseshoes to horses' feet, in the early part of the twentieth century horseshoe nails were sometimes bent into circles to produce rings that were very popular with rural grade school children.

Horseweed   An annual common throughout North America. It grows as high as six feet and during the Depression years of the 1930s was sometimes pulled up and fed to livestock.

Hot blood   A term used to describe a type of hog popular in the 1880s. Such hogs were short-bodied, short-legged, had barrel-shaped bodies, and were early maturing.

Hot chisel   See **Hot set**.

Hot set   A chisel with a wooden handle that looks much like a hammer, except that there is a chisel on the end where claws would normally be. Blacksmiths used such chisels when cutting hot metal. The long handle kept the blacksmith from being burned.

Hotbed   A heated bed of soil used for early planting of vegetables. Heating was usually from buried decaying animal waste.

Hound   Part of a wagon. See **Hawn**.

Hub boxing. The conical, tubular steel or malleable iron bearing that fits inside the wooden hub of a wagon wheel and over the **Skein**.

Hudson   The Hudson Motor Car Company of Detroit, MI was formed in 1909, and was initially financed by J. L. Hudson of Detroit. In 1954, it combined with Nash to form American Motors.

Hupmobile   An automobile made in Detroit from 1908 to 1940. Robert and Louis Hupp founded the company.

Husker   See **Corn husker**.

I

Ice house   (1) A building where ice was stored. When the only source of ice was that frozen during the winter months, ice was often harvested and stored in heavily insulated ice houses for use during the summer. (2) Later, a place where ice was manufactured.

Ice tongs   When iceboxes were used that required blocks of ice for cooling, ice was gen-erally sold in blocks weighing 25, 50, or 100 pounds. Ice tongs were used to grip those blocks when they were to be moved.

Icebox   The common name for an insulated cabinet that used blocks of ice to keep food stored in the cabinet cool. Since ice was only available to those rural inhabitants who lived in climates where ice could be harvested and stored in the winter for later use in the summer, iceboxes had only limited rural usage.   The then current dictionaries referred to such insulated boxes not as iceboxes but, rather, as refrigerators. Those who grew up in the "icebox" era often referred to electric refrigerators as iceboxes.

Iceless refrigerator   A cabinet for holding food that had screenwire sides and a covering of porous cloth. The cloth was kept wet by being dipped in a pan of water. The water evaporating kept the cabinet cool. Evaporative cooling was the only kind of cooling possible when ice was not available and was also sometimes used for keeping drinking water cool. It was not, for example, uncommon to take a fruit jar filled with drinking water and wrapped with a damp gunnysack to the field each summer day.   When a recirculating refrigerant began being used rather than a block of ice for cooling (i.e. the refrigerator of today), the machines were sometimes called iceless refrigerators.

Illuminating gas   See **Artificial gas**.

Incubator   A box-like structure with insulation and provisions for controlling its interior temperature. The incubator is used for hatching chicken, turkey, duck, or goose eggs. Before the availability of electricity to farms, coal oil lamps were used to heat water circulating by convection through pipes around the perimeter of the brooder. A thermostat caused a damper to open and close and either trap or let hot air escape from the lamp chimney.

Indian corn   At the beginning of the twentieth century the term Indian corn was still used by some to refer to what is now called corn but, in some locales, the name Indian corn was applied only to those ears with red or blue kernels that were occasionally found mixed in with the more usual yellow or white kernels. Such colors are not found when hybrid seed corn is used.

Indian peaches   A name applied to small white-fleshed peaches sometimes found around abandoned farmhouse sites. Such peaches probably grew on suckers from the original rootstock after the peach variety grafted onto the rootstock had died from neglect. The name Indian peach was used even though peaches are not native to the Americas.

Indian rattlebox   A geode containing loose sand particles that rattle when the geode is shaken.

Indian stomp dance   A male Indian dance characterized by foot stamping. The dance was usually to give thanks for some event, e.g., the green corn stomp dance celebrating the beginning of a good crop of corn.

Indian Territory   Roughly, the Eastern half of what is now the state of Oklahoma. In 1907, Oklahoma Territory and Indian Territory were combined to form the state of Oklahoma. Indian Territory was mainly occupied by the five Civilized Tribes, comprised of the Cherokee Nation, the Chickasaw Nation, the Choctaw Nation, the Creek Nation, and the Seminole Nation.

Infants' binder   See **Belly button band**.

Insecticide sprinkler   Instead of spraying water-based insecticides, sprinklers were sometimes used. The insecticide was not under pressure, but rather just dripped out from a tank onto the growing plants. Such dispensers were sometimes called "potato bug sprinklers" because their most common application was for controlling potato bugs.

Isinglass   A transparent gelatin made from the bladder of certain fish and used to make glue. Isinglass was also a term applied to the thin, transparent sheets of mica used in wood- and coal-burning stove door windows. When thin sheets of clear plastic first began to be used for such things as vehicle window curtains, they were also sometimes referred to as being of isinglass.

J

Jack   (1) A small six-pronged object used in the game of jacks, a game widely played by girls in the 1930s. In the early part of the twentieth century such jacks were generally of metal but, by the twenty-first century, were usually plastic. (2) A male donkey. The first jack in the U.S. was sent to George Washington by King Charles III of Spain. (3) An instrument for raising a heavy weight a short distance.

Jack pen   A small pen built in a barn and used for holding a **Jack** (number 2). Jacks, sometimes kept for breeding, were often very mean-tempered and, in the confines of a barn, needed to be kept separated from the other farm animals.

Jack screw   A **Jack** (number 3) with a heavy CAST IRON base and a large screw that can be turned to raise or lower a load.

Jacks   A children's' game played with a small ball and several jacks (see **Jack**, number 1).

Jamaica train   A row of iron kettles (usually three) used to boil cane juice (sugar cane for making sugar, sorghum for making molasses).

Jax   A contraction sometimes used when referring to the game of **Jacks**.

Jennet   A female donkey. Sometimes shortened to **Jenny**.

Jenny   A female donkey, but it was also a name sometimes applied to female MULES.

K

Kafir or kafir-corn   A variety of sorghum. Old textbooks some-times listed kafir-corn as being separate from the sorghums.

Kalsomine   A thin whitewash composed primarily of Paris white and water. It was sometimes used instead of the more expensive paint to cover walls and fences, and was said to pre-vent mites when painted on the inside of chicken houses.

Keeler   A shallow tub.

Kerosene   See **Coal oil**.

Keystone Manufacturing Co.   An early farm implement manufacturer.

Kicker chain   A chain used around a milk cow's hind legs to keep her from kicking while being milked. It was needed only on cows that had not yet become used to being milked.

Kicking the can   Kicking the can (or kicking the bucket) was a game played by boys during school recess. Despite its name, no mayhem was involved. A circle a few feet in diameter was drawn in the dirt, and the "it" person stayed in the circle with his foot on a can or old bucket while everyone else hid anywhere on the school grounds except in the school building itself. "It" looked around, and anyone he could see was "captured" and placed inside the circle. When all the obvious people were captured, he then had to leave his can and move away from the circle to look for the other participants. If one of those not captured could run up and kick the unattended can out of the circle, everyone in the circle was set free. If, however, "It" could dash back and get his foot on the can before it was kicked out of the circle, the would-be kicker was captured and had to stay inside the circle. The game ended either when everyone was captured or when recess was over.

Kingpin   A large iron pin that went through the front wagon bolster and coupling pole and into the front wagon axle.

Knickerbocker pants   Pants with legs long enough to reach a short distance below the knees. When worn, however, the pant leg ends were constrained to remain just below the knees. This gave a ballooned appearance to the end of the pant legs. Knickerbocker pants were sometimes worn by boys and young men and women, although the style was most often associated with golf players.

Knickerbockers   See **Knickerbocker pants**.

Knickers   Short for **Knickerbocker pants**.

Knife handle wrench   A name sometimes used for a **Monkey wrench**.

Knife rest   A small, short, rod-like support of glass, china, or metal that was laid to the right of plates and used to keep dirty knife blades from touching the tablecloth.

L

Lady's rocking chair   A rocking chair charac-terized by a straight back and no arms. Such chairs were sometimes called sewing chairs because it is easier to hand-sew in a chair without arms. They were also sometimes called nursing chairs because it was easier to hold a baby if one sat in a chair without arms.

Lambs quarter   A wild plant sometimes used in salads.

Lamp Chimney   The glass enclosure around the flame of a coal oil light. It kept wind from blowing out the flame and provided a means for the hot air from the flame to rise and draw fresh air into the lamp and flame.

Land roller   See **Dirt roller**.

Landside   The part of a turning plow that slides along the face of the furrow wall. (That wall defines the edge of the furrow.)

Lap robe   A blanket used to keep one's feet and legs warm while riding in a wagon or buggy.

Lard   Rendered hog fat.

Larding needle   A large needle used to insert strings of lard into lean meat to improve flavor.

La Salle   The La Salle was a car made by the Cadillac Motor Car Company. It was manufactured from 1927 until 1940.

Last   See **Shoe last**.

Last stand   See **Shoe last** discussion.

Laudanum   Laudanum was a painkiller containing opium and could be openly purchased without a prescription in any drug store.

Laying by   The last CULTIVATION plowing of the season. By that time, the crop plants were beginning to be too high to plow without breaking down some of the stalks and, for the rest of the year, the crop was big enough to outgrow any additional weeds that might start growing.

Leaf lard   The lard found next to the kidneys and generally considered to be the best.

Leghorn   (1) A breed of chicken. (2) A hat made of straw from an Italian wheat. Such hats were generally for women and were wide-brimmed and flat-topped. The name came from Leghorn, Italy.

Leghorn hat   See second definition of **Leghorn**.

Lever power   A **Horse power**.

Lid Lifter   See **Stove lid lifter**.

Liebig's beef tea   A tea considered good for the sick. It was made by boiling one pound of lean beef, finely chopped, with one pint of water, then straining.

Lights   The lungs of slaughtered calves and pigs. They were sometimes eaten shortly after butchering and were considered by some to be a delicacy and by others to be just another organ meat that should not be wasted.

Linen collar   A detachable shirt collar made of linen that could easily be removed and washed when dirty and thus extend the time between shirt washings.

Linen cuff A detachable shirt cuff made of linen that could easily be removed and washed when dirty and thus extend the time between shirt washings.

Lines Long leather straps about an inch wide running from the horse's (or mule's) bridle to the driver. When a line broke, a long piece of rope was sometimes temporarily substituted for the leather line. Another temporary fix was just to tie the line together, but the permanent fix was to rivet the ends of the broken line together.

Link A unit of length, being one link of a surveyor's chain, or 7.92 inches (0.66 ft.).

Linseed tea Made by boiling linseed (flaxseed) and various flavorings in water, straining, and then sweetening. Sometimes additional flavoring such as lemon juice or licorice were added to make the tea more palatable. Linseed tea was used to combat bladder infections.

Linsey Same as **Linsey-woolsey**.

Linsey-woolsey A coarse fabric made of mixed wool and linen.

Liquid smoke By the end of the twentieth century liquid smoke was a meat flavoring or marinade, but in the early part of the century it was a liquid meat preservative sometimes used as an alternative to actual meat smoking.

Lister To some, a plow with two MOLDBOARDS arranged so that, as a furrow is plowed, the dirt is thrown half to the right and half to the left. To others, a lister was the plow just described combined with a planter. Those who used the latter terminology often referred to the first plow as a **Middlebreaker**, **Middlebuster**, or **Ridge buster**. However, the term **Ridge buster** was also sometimes used instead of **Go-devil**.

Lister cultivator A CULTIVATOR designed expressly for crops planted in deep lister furrows.

Lister planter A planter designed specifically to plant in a listed furrow. The deep furrow planting that was applicable to drier geographical regions used a lister (double-MOLDBOARD plow) to make the deep furrow needed. Early planters consisted of a planter mechanism attached to a walking lister and driven by two spiked wheels riding in the furrow. Later, a planter mechanism was combined with one- and two-row riding listers to produce what was referred to as a lister planter. See also the **Lister** discussion.

Log chain Stout chain used for tying heavy loads to a wagon and for hitching a team to an implement or automobile that needed to be to be pulled from the mud.

Log saw See **Drag saw**.

London purple An insecticide used primarily for orchard insects. Its active ingredient was calcium arsenate, which is white but, in the early twentieth century, calcium arsenate was sometimes obtained as a by-product of the aniline dye industry and had a purple hue.

Long handles   See **Long johns**.

Long johns   One-piece mens' and boys' underwear that buttoned down the front (union suits).

Lye soap   Soap made by reacting lye with beef tallow or lard.

M

Macadam road   A road surfaced according to the Macadam plan. That plan called for first spreading and rolling a three- or four-inch layer of coarse rocks of uniform size on a graded roadway and then covering it with a layer of finely crushed rock that was worked down into the interstices of the first layer.

Mackinaw   (1) A heavy blanket formerly supplied to Indians of the Northwest by the US Government. (2) A coat made of mackinaw-like material.

Mackintosh   A waterproof overcoat. Originally a rainproof coat made by laminating two pieces of cotton cloth using a solution of rubber and naphtha. The process was invented by Charles Macintosh and patented in 1823.

Magic eye   See **Tuning eye**.

Maize   Corn.

Margarine   See **Oleomargarine**.

Martingale   A leather strap attached at one end to a **Girth**, then running between the front legs of a horse and up to the **Bridle bit**, and used to control the upper movement of the horse's head. It was primarily used with saddled horses and not with harness and workhorses.

Maxwell   The Maxwell automobile (1894–1925) was originally made by the Maxwell-Briscoe Motor Company of Newcastle, Indiana, then by the Maxwell Motor Corporation (Detroit, MI). Walter Chrysler took control of that company in 1923, introduced a Chrysler in 1924, and had phased out the Maxwell name by 1926.

McCormick Harvesting Machine Company   An early manufacturer of reapers. It was incorporated in 1879, but some McCormick had been making reapers since Cyrus McCormick invented a successful one in 1831.

Metz   An automobile made by the Metz Company of Waltham, Massachusetts from 1909 until 1922. Their first vehicles were sold in kit form for home assembly. Until the last year of their manufacture, they used a variable speed friction drive instead of a conventional transmission.

Michigan double plow   This plow had two bottoms inline, with the one behind arranged to plow in the furrow left by the first bottom. The final furrow was thus much deeper than could be plowed by a single bottom of the same width.

Middlebreaker   See **Lister** discussion.

Middlebuster   See **Lister** discussion.

Milk can   A sturdy galvanized steel can with a
tight-fitting lid. Such cans were used for storing
milk and cream and for shipping them by train.
Because of the latter use, they were sometimes
called railway milk cans. Five gallon and ten gallon
sizes were common.

Milk pie   A Depression-era pie with a filling of milk, sugar, a
little flour, and some vanilla flavoring.

Milk stool   A short stool used to sit on while milking. While
milk stools are usually shown as short three-legged stools, they
often had only one leg and were made from lumber scraps, e.g.
a ten-inch length of 2 × 6 nailed to a short section of 4 × 4 or
firewood. That one leg, along with the two of the milker, comprised a stable support.

Milk sugar   A form of sugar found in mammals' milk and now
usually referred to as lactose. When an infant had to be bottle-
fed, cows' milk was sometimes fortified with extra milk sugar.

Milo   A high-yield grain sorghum.

Milt   Another name for the spleen, an organ meat sometimes
eaten.

Model A   (1) The first automobile model introduced by the Ford Motor Co. (2) The Ford Motor Co. model that in 1928 replaced the **Model T**. This model had a forty horsepower engine and was a much more conventional automobile than the **Model T** which, by the time it was replaced, was considered by many to be obsolete.

Model T   An inexpensive and easy to maintain automobile introduced by Henry Ford and the Ford Motor Co. in 1908. The first Ford Motor Co. automobile, however, was a Model A, introduced in 1903. It had a two-cylinder, eight-horsepower engine, wooden wheels, a two forward speed transmission and was not *the* Model A introduced as a successor to the Model T. Between the original Model A and the Model T there were the Models B, C, F, K, N, R, and S. The Model T still had wooden wheels, but a substantial four-cylinder engine, a separate coil for each cylinder spark plug, and no electric starter. It also had electric lights powered by a magneto. Ford pioneered the use of high-strength alloy steel, and cast-off Model T rear axles were much favored as a source of steel for farm repair work. Even though the engine was substantially more powerful than that on previous models, it was still sometimes necessary to back up hills, since reverse had a lower gear ratio than the forward low gear. Another reason sometimes cited for backing up hills was that if the gas tank was low on fuel, going uphill in a forward direction would tilt the tank so much that fuel would not feed to the carburetor.

Molasses   A term now applied to the residual syrup from sugarmaking but, in farming communities, "molasses" meant the boiled-down juice of sweet sorghum cane.

Moldboard   Sometimes used as short for a **Mold-board plow (Walking turning plow)**. See also MOLDBOARD.

Moldboard plow   A colloquial term for a **Walking turning plow**.

Monitor Drill Company   A farm implement manufacturer.

Monkey   A colloquial expression for a one-horse plow-like implement used to hook and pull up cane stalks by their roots, also see **Water monkey**.

Monkey wrench   One of the few types of wrenches found on most early twentieth-century farms. Its jaws were at right angles to the handle. One jaw was adjustable. The other, much heavier and at the end of the handle, was often used as a hammer. Charles Moncky apparently invented the wrench sometime before 1860.

Moss jelly   A jelly made from moss. The jelly had little nutritional value, but was still considered good for the sick. Depending on the kind of moss (e.g., Iceland moss), the procedure for making the jelly varied somewhat, but generally about an ounce of dried moss was boiled in a quart of water and, after a substantial amount of water had boiled away, the remainder was strained through a sieve. Flavoring or a little milk was added if desired.

Mother-in-law seat   See **Rumble seat**.

Mother of vinegar A cluster of the bacteria that converts alcohol to vinegar. When vinegar for household use was bought or made in multiple-gallon quantities, it might stay in a wooden barrel or cask for several months. During that time, the mother of vinegar would sometimes grow into gelatinous masses several inches across.

Motor court Motel, also see **Tourist court**.

Mountain boomer A term sometimes used by children for a collared lizard.

Mouthbow See **Songbow**.

Muley A dictionary definition is "naturally hornless," and indeed hornless cows, particularly hornless old milk cows, were sometimes called muleys. However, the term was also applied to other things that appeared to be missing some feature. One example was the muley CULTIVATOR, which was a horse-drawn cultivator designed to not have a tongue.

Music bow or **musical bow** See **Songbow**.

N

Nail A linear measurement used for cloth. It equals 2.25 inches.

Nappie Same as **Nappy**.

Nappy A shallow dish with sloping sides and a flat bottom used for cooking or serving food.

Nash An automobile named after Charles W. Nash, made by the Nash Motor Company of Kenosha, WI from 1917 until 1954, and by the American Motor Company from 1954 through 1957.

Near horse The left horse of a pair, as the left horse of a two-horse team.

Neat's-foot oil An oil used in making a preparation for keeping harness leather from cracking. Neat refers to bovines, and neat's-foot oil is obtained by boiling the shinbones and feet of butchered cattle.

Neck yoke A wooden beam or pole about three feet long with specialized iron fittings on each end and at the middle. (See **Neck yoke attachment** and **Neck yoke ferrule and ring**.) The **Tongue** of the implement to be pulled was attached to the middle of the yoke, and one of the yoke ends was attached to the hames of the harness of the horse on that side of the tongue. The other end of the yoke was similarly attached to the hames of the horse on the other side of the tongue.

Neck yoke attachment A large iron ring with two eyebolts and two reinforcement plates. The assembly was bolted to the center of a neck yoke. The ring fitted over the **Pole cap** on the end of an implement tongue.

Neck yoke ferrule and ring A ferrule was fitted on each end of a neck yoke. The attached ring was then used to connect the yoke to harness. Also, see **Neck yoke**.

Neck yoke strap   See **Pole strap**.

Nest egg   Nest eggs, usually made of wood, porcelain, or celluloid, were put in hens' nests to promote egg laying. The idea being that if a hen saw an egg (real or artificial) already in a nest she would be more likely to lay one herself.

Nobby   Elegant or stylish.

Normal school   A college (usually only two years) for preparing students to become schoolteachers who could then teach through the eighth grade.

Nursing chair   See **Lady's rocking chair**.

O

Ocarina   A small, simple musical wind instrument with a body shaped something like a sweet potato.

Odd-row Monitor   A two-row lister CULTIVATOR designed so the horses walked between adjacent rows, but there was a row between the two rows being plowed. The every-other-row feature, combined with the name Monitor Drill Company (one of the manufacturers) gave rise to the name of "odd-row monitor."

Oil of vitriol   Sulphuric acid.

Oleo   When "margarine" was referred to by its original full name of oleomargarine, it was often just called "oleo" for short.

Oleo oil   A thick, yellowish oil obtained from some animal fats, e.g., from high-quality beef tallow.

Oleomargarine   The original name of what is now called margarine.

One-horse cultivator   An implement for CULTIVATION that was narrow enough to go between rows, generally had either five or fourteen teeth or small **Shovels**, and was pulled by one horse. Often its width could be adjusted by changing the separation of the teeth or **Shovels**.

One-way plow   See **Hillside plow**.

Osage orange   Another name for the bois d'arc tree.

Outlaw rule   One of several formulas, and one that is generally grossly inaccurate, for estimating the volume of haystacks. Despite the inaccuracy, this rule was widely used in the Midwest. First, measure the distance from the ground on one side of the stack over the stack and down to the ground on the other side. Multiply that number by the stack width, divide the product by four, and multiply by the stack length to get the volume in cubic feet. For other formulae, see the **Fowl rule**, the **Frye-Bruhn rule**, and the **Quartermaster's** rule.

Overland   An automobile made by the Overland Co. of Indianapolis, IN from 1905–1907, and later by the Willys-Overland Company of Toledo, OH.

Ox   A large steer used as a draft animal. Oxen were used much earlier than horses for agricultural work, and when they began to lose substantial ground to horses is not clear. In North American colonial times, cattle were more valued for draft purposes than as a source of meat. Stagecoaches, however, were pulled by horses, since there the emphasis was on speed. The covered freight wagons that moved westward were, for the most part, pulled by oxen. The use of oxen survived in the U.S. into the twentieth century and, in some parts of the world, oxen are still being used in the twenty-first century.

Ox bow   (1) The part of an ox **Yoke** that fitted around the ox's neck. The bow was made of a wooden pole (usually hickory), about an inch in diameter and bent into a U shape. (2) A curve in a river that is shaped somewhat like the bow described in (1).

Ox claw   A name sometimes used for one-half of the cloven hoof of an ox.

Ox shoes   Iron plates nailed to the bottom of an ox's hooves to protect the hooves from wear when the ox was being used as a draft animal. Since oxen have cloven hooves, two plates are required per hoof.

Ox shovel   Same as a **Slip**.

Ox yoke   See **Yoke**.

P

P   Colloquial term for the **Poise** used on **Cotton scales**. For an illustration, see **Poise** entry.

Packard   Packard automobiles were first made by two Packard brothers in 1899. Packards continued to be made through 1958, although by then they were manufactured by the Studebaker-Packard Company. From 1903 through 1958, the companies were located in Detroit, MI.

Paint pot   A container for holding paint while painting. The original paint container could not necessarily be used because barn and house paints were sometimes sold in twenty-five or fifty-gallon barrels.

Paint pot hook   A hook used to hang paint pots from a ladder rung.

Paris green   An insecticide composed of copper acetoarsenite. It is an emerald green powder that is insoluble in water.

Paris white   Calcium carbonate. It is a major constituent of **Kalsomine**.

Parlin & Orendorff Co.   A farm implement manufacturer, founded in 1842 to make plows.

Part   A unit of surface measurement that is twelve inches long and one inch wide, i.e., $\frac{1}{12}$ of a square foot.

Pastry board   See **Breadboard**.

Peaked   Sickly-looking.

Peck   A unit of volume measure. One peck is two gallons, or ¼ bushel.

Peck sack   A sack, usually paper, holding ¼ bushel (two gallons). Vegetables were often sold by the peck.

Peg awl   An awl, mostly used by shoemakers, for making holes in shoes for shoe pegs.

Perch   A unit of measure. For linear measurement, 1 perch=1 rod (5.5 yds). When applied to masonry, 1 perch=24.75 cubic feet.

Phaeton   A light four-wheeled carriage. Both sides of the carriage were open in front of the seats.

Phosphate   A soft drink made by mixing **Acid phosphate** and a fruit-flavored syrup.

Pie bird   A hollow ceramic bird-shaped figurine about three inches high, with openings at the top and bottom, that could be set with its base below the surface of a pie crust before baking to prevent steam build-up under the top crust during baking. Puncturing the pie top with a fork before baking removes the need of the pie bird.

Pie safe A box-like enclosure for storing and protecting pies from mice and insects. The safes ranged in size from those containing only one or two shelves, three or so feet long, up to six-foot high cupboards. Air circulation was provided by safe wall or door sections of metal perforated by many tiny holes.

Pie supper A combination social and fundraising event in which girls or young single women brought pies that were sold by auction. The purchaser and the original pie owner then shared the pie. Proceeds generally went to either church or school needs.

Pierce Arrow The first model of this automobile was built by George N. Pierce in 1901. The last one was built in 1938. Company headquarters were in Buffalo, NY.

Pig nuts A bitter, thin-shelled hickory nut much liked by hogs.

Pigweed An annual that grows along fence rows, at the end of crop rows, and on other wasteland. The redroot variety may grow several feet tall and, during the Depression years of the 1930s, was sometimes pulled up as feed for livestock. Depending on the mineral content of the soil, the pigweed may be poisonous to cattle.

Pinafore A full-length apron to protect the front of a girl's dress. Pinafores were usually very plain, but sometimes mothers would embellish them with colored tape (as was the one on the little girl shown here) or other simple decorations.

Pindar   Regional term for peanut. Apparently, the term was not much used past the nineteenth century.

Pintsch gas   See **Artificial gas**.

Pipe   A unit of liquid volume. One pipe equals two **Hogsheads**.

Pitcher pump   A simply designed shallow well pump with an open spout that looks much like that of a pitcher. When a shallow well or a cistern were either next to the house or under it, a pitcher pump was often located in the kitchen next to the sink.

Pitless scale   Part of the mechanism of wagon scales was normally in a pit so that the scale platform was at ground level and a wagon could easily be pulled onto it. However, some scales were built so that the entire mechanism was only a few inches thick and, by using a small incline, a loaded wagon could still be pulled onto the scale even when the scale was totally on top of the ground and the wagon was heavily loaded.

Pitman rod   Connecting rod used to convert from rotation to reciprocating motion. A Pitman rod was used, for example, on a MOWING MACHINE to drive the reciprocating SICKLE BAR. They were generally made of wood so that if there were a jam, the wood (easily replaceable) would break before any of the other machinery was bent or broken.

Plank gum   See **Gum**.

Plant-setting machine   See **transplanter**.

Platform scales   For items that were not of a convenient shape to be weighed on cotton scales, e.g. sacks of feed, platform scales were used. They looked much like the scales to be found in a doctor's office except that they were much more heavily constructed and had a larger platform.

Plow clevis   A pair of iron plates clamped onto the end of a walking plow beam and having a series of holes spaced vertically in them. By then adding other kinds of clevises, such as the crosslink clevis shown in the figure, an evener could be attached to the plow. Depending on which holes were used in the plow clevis, the plowing depth could be varied.

Plow pan   See **Hardpan**.

Plow point   A term often used instead of PLOWSHARE. Also, see PLOW SHOVEL.

Plowsole   See **Hardpan**.

Plug (of tobacco)   A small, flat, rectangular-shaped cake of compressed chewing tobacco. Pieces of a size suitable for chewing (a **Chaw**) could then be cut off as desired.

Plunge churn   See **Dasher churn**.

Plunger churn   See **Dasher churn**.

Poise   Counterbalance weight for **Cotton scales**. A poise might weigh from a fraction of a pound to thirty or more pounds. It was more commonly referred to as a **P**.

Poke   (1) A sack. (2) A plant that's leaves are sometimes used for salad. (3) Also, see **Cow poke**.

Poke salad   Cooked leaves of the poke plant. The raw leaves are generally considered poisonous, and are thus boiled in several changes of water before eating.

Poke salet   See **Poke salad**.

Poker   A metal rod about two feet long with a handle on one end and a right angle bend on the other. Pokers were used to stir burning wood or coal in stoves.

Pole   See **Buggy pole**.

Pole cap   An iron fitting put on the end of a tongue to hold a **Neck yoke** in place.

Pole strap   A part of harness that consisted of a leather strap with a loop on one end. When an implement with a tongue was being pulled, the neck yoke went through the loop. The other end of the strap went between the horse's front legs and was connected to the breeching by other straps. With this arrangement, the horses could pull back on the implement and either apply braking or cause the implement to back up. Sometimes, the pole strap was extended up to the bridle so that the combination could function as both a pole strap and a martingale. Such combinations were sometimes called neck yoke martingales.

Polecat   Polecat is the common name for a weasel-like carnivore, but colloquially it referred to a skunk.

Porcelain ware   Some utensils such as teapots were made of porcelain, but such pots would, of course, crack if heated on the stove. (If an enamelware utensil was overheated, as could happen if a **Teakettle** boiled dry, the enamel coating would also crack and flake off.) Usually, a "porcelain" utensil really meant a utensil of enamelware.

Post drill   A hand-operated drill press for drilling in metal. It had a crank, flywheel, and positive feed. The various parts were mounted on a wooden timber that was in turn mounted on a wall or post.

Post maul   A heavy sledgehammer with two identical flat faces. Where the dirt was free of rocks and relatively soft, the post maul was used to drive pointed wood fence posts into the ground.

Postillion   One who rides the near horse of a team in order to guide the team. Such riders were found on teams hauling artillery and were sometimes used by the wealthy to guide their coach teams, but were not used in conjunction with farm implements. Sometimes a small boy would ride one horse of a team when doing something like harrowing, but in general, the implements themselves required attention while being pulled so the operator did the double duty of operating the equipment and guiding the team. Also, while a harnessed horse would generally tolerate a rider, workhorses were not necessarily broken for riding, and trying to ride an unharnessed plow horse could be disastrous.

Pot cheese   Very similar to cottage cheese, except that it was drier.

Presser wheel   A wide-rimmed wheel at the back of a seed planter to press down and compact the dirt covering the seeds.

Prest-O-Lite®   Acetylene gas supplied in a small tank under an initial pressure of about 15 atmospheres. The gas was burned in early automobile headlights. When the tank was empty, it could be exchanged for a full one.

Prime $\frac{1}{12}$ of a square foot.

Prince Albert can   A small metal can that originally held Prince Albert tobacco. Empty cans were often used by small boys for storing such items as fish hooks.

Proud flesh   The outward uncontrolled growth of flesh from a wound such as a blister worn on a horse's neck by a poorly fitting collar, an improper attachment position of the trace chains to the hames, or overwork. One cure was to treat the growth with copper sulfate.

Pump action churn   See **Dasher churn**.

Pump jack   A machine that could be attached to a water well pump designed to be used with a windmill that could allow the pump to be operated by a gasoline engine.

Punch   Same as paunch or stomach.

Push binder   A small-grain binder designed such that the horses walked behind the SICKLE BAR and **Reel**, rather than beside them.

Push plow   GARDEN PLOW.

Q

Quarter   A unit of weight. One quarter equals 25 pounds (80 qr./ton).

Quartermaster's rule   One of several formulas for estimating the volume of haystacks, and one of the more accurate. First, add together the width of the stack and the distance from the ground on one side of the stack, over the stack and down to the ground on the other side. Then, divide that number by four, square the result, and multiply the result by the length of the stack to give the volume of the stack in cubic feet. For other formulae, see the **Fowl rule**, the **Frye-Bruhn rule**, and the **Outlaw rule**.

R

Railroad milk can   See **Milk can**.

Railway power   A **Treadmill**.

Rain barrel   A barrel used to catch rainwater running off roofs. The main reason for saving rainwater was because it was soft and worked well for washing hair and clothes. See SOFT WATER.

Range   (1) A region used for livestock grazing. (2) Often used interchangeably with "cook stove," but sometimes implying a large cook stove, and sometimes meaning a cook stove with a shelf or warming oven above the main stove surface.

Razorback   A thin, long-legged feral hog, most generally found in the hills of the Southeastern US.

Razor strap   See **Strop**.

Razor strop   See **Strop**.

REA   Acronym for the Rural Electrification Act, which was originally put in place in 1935, then modified and extended in 1936, to speed the extension of power lines to rural areas.

Reach   See **Coupling pole**.

Ready reckoner   See **Reckoner**.

Reaper   An implement to cut stalks of grain and leave them on the ground in untied bundles. Early machines required a man walking alongside the reaper to rake the bundles off the collecting platform and onto the ground. Later models had provisions for one or two men to ride on the reaper.

Reckoner   A small book of assorted tables that was mainly used by store owners who did not want to take the time to do the necessary arithmetic, or by those who did not know how to do the calculations. Included were tables such as interest amount vs. time and rate, board dimensions vs. board feet, and cistern capacity vs. cistern dimensions.

Reckoning machine   A mechanical calculator.

Red root   A large, reddish mass of gnarled and hard roots sometimes found in unbroken prairie.

Reel   The part of a **Header** or **Small-grain binder** used to move the heads or cut stalks of grain onto a canvas conveyor belt.

Refrigerator   In the early twentieth century, a refrigerator was what would now be called an **Icebox**. That is, an insulated cabinet that used blocks of ice to keep food stored in the cabinet cool.

Reins   See **Lines**.

Rench   To strain a liquid.

REO   A car made by the REO Car Company of Lansing, MI from 1904 through 1936. The name REO came from the initials of Ransom E. Olds, founder of the company.

Rice water   Made by steeping rice in warm water, boiling, and adding flavoring if desired. Said to be helpful for diarrhea.

Rick   (1) Half a cord of firewood. (2) A stack of sticks of firewood or other wood that is 8 feet long, 4 feet high, and as deep as the length of the sticks. (3) A small stack of hay.

Ridge buster   A **Middlebuster**. See also the **Lister** discussion.

Rige   To strain a liquid.

Rive   To split, often applied to the splitting of logs into thin sections for planks or shingles.

River bottom   See **Creek bottom**.

Roach   To trim a horse's mane short enough that it stands up straight.

Rocky Mountain brake   Before brakes were available on wagons, a little sled was often carried along in the wagon and placed under a wheel to increase drag when going downhill. The sled was attached to the wagon with a short piece of chain in such a manner that, when properly positioned, the sled was always dragged along under the wheel. This approach was continued after conventional wagon brakes became available, and in the U.S., was often referred to as Rocky Mountain brakes.

Rod   A unit of length measure, equal to 16.5 feet, and often used when measuring land or fencing. A quarter-mile is 80 rods in length, as is a spool of barbed wire.

Rod breaker   Same as **Rod plow**.

Rod plow   Sometimes called a **Sod-cutting plow**; it was a **Walking turning plow** in which the MOLD-BOARD consisted of a few steel rods. Such plows were particularly adapted to turning unbroken prairie.

Rod weeder   An implement that dragged a rod just beneath the surface of plowed and HARROWED ground to pull out small weeds.

Rolley holley   A marble game with rules much like those of croquet, except that a marble shooter and marble replaced the croquet mallet and ball, and small holes in the ground in an L pattern replaced the wickets.

Rolls razor   A razor introduced in the 1920s that had the hoe design of a safety razor, but was really only a single-edge blade and a handle that could be clamped onto the blade. However, the blade did not have as much protective shielding as a typical safety razor, and shaving with a Rolls required about as much care as when using a straight razor. The protection it did have prevented deep cuts, but not shallow ones. The main advantage of the Rolls was that it came in a storage box that incorporated a blade sharpening mechanism consisting of an integral **Whetstone**, **Strop**, and track with a blade holder. The blade holder positioned the blade at an optimum angle for sharpening, and also reversed the side of the blade presented to the stone or strop, as the blade and its holder were pushed back and forth along the track. Using the sharpening feature, a single blade could be sharpened and used many times.

Rooter (1) Another name for a hog's snout. (2) Sometimes used colloquially to mean a whole, live hog.

Rotation or **Centrifugal seeder** Same as a **Rotation** or **Centrifugal sower**.

Rotation sower Any seeder working like the **End-gate seeder**, i.e., one that scattered seeds by dropping them onto a rotating disk.

Row binder An implement to travel along a crop row, cut, and then tie the stalks into bundles. More often called a **Corn binder**, it traveled down a single row, cut off the stalks and kept them upright until after they were tied into a bundle. The bundles were either shocked and left in the field, or stored in a barn.

Row planter See **Corn planter**.

Rub board A term sometimes used instead of **Washboard**.

Rug beater See **Carpet beater**.

Rumble seat Originally a seat for servants behind the main body of a carriage, but later an uncovered folding automobile seat placed where the trunk is now located. The rumble seat was also sometimes referred to as a **Mother-in-law seat**.

Running gear   One of the major components of a horse-drawn wagon. It consisted of the wheels, axles, hawns, tongue, bolsters, and coupling pole (reach). See the **Hawns** entry for a sketch of the running gear.

S

Sacque   An infant's short jacket that fastens at the neck.

Saddle soap   A mild soap, usually containing extra oil, used for cleaning leather.

Sadiron   A **Flatiron** pointed at both ends and having a removable handle. Usually the irons were sold in groups of three, along with one handle. Such irons had no internal heating element and were usually heated on top of the kitchen stove. While one iron and its handle was being used for ironing, the other two could be heating on the stove.

Sago   A drink for the sick made by dissolving a spoonful of sago starch in a cup of hot water.

Salt   While salt usually meant sodium chloride used as a food seasoning and as a food preservative, it sometimes referred to a small salt container. Same as a **Table salt**.

Saltspoon   A small spoon holding one-fourth teaspoon and used for dipping salt from a **Table salt**.

Samp   Boiled corn that had been cracked (ground) to a size coarser than that used for conventional cornmeal.

Sand board   A part of wagon **Running gear**. See **Bolster** for more discussion.

Sandrock   Same as **Sandstone**.

Sarsaparilla   (Ordinarily pronounced sas'-pa-ril'-a.) A beverage flavoring or a tea made from the dried root of the *smilax medica chamisso*, which is found in Jamaica, Honduras, Mexico, Brazil, and Guatemala.

Sassafras tea   Sassafras tea is made by boiling the roots or bark of the sassafras tree in water. The tea was a widely used tonic and was considered an important medicine for thinning and purifying the blood. The sassafras tree, sometimes referred to as the Ague tree, is a member of the laurel family, and is native to North America.

Sausage stuffer   A small hand press used to force sausage into a casing.

Sawhorse   While there were sawhorses used by carpenters for holding boards for sawing, a "sawhorse" was usually intended to hold a small log as the log was being sawed into short lengths for firewood.

Scalding vat   A vat, containing hot water, that was used during hog butchering. One of the early steps in hog butchering was to immerse the carcass for a few minutes in boiling water (the scalding vat) to loosen the hair. For more details, see **Hog scraper**. On large, well-established farms, the vat might be placed over a fire so the water could be kept hot. In addition, since butchering was always done during cold weather, the vat might be located in a small building. On small farms, the water was commonly heated in a large kettle and then put in a barrel tilted so that a hog could be easily slid into it, but still hold enough hot water to allow the hog carcass to be scalded. Some indoor installations also had a pulley or windlass arraignment so that a hog could be easily lifted out of the vat.

Scale beam   See **Cotton scale**. Scale beams worked on the same principle as **Steelyards**, but instead of having the straight beam of a steelyard, scale beams had an upward curve to the beam on the side of the pivot away from the poise location.

Scallop   See **Scallop plate**.

Scallop plate   A plate in the shape of a scallop shell. Scalloped oysters, at one time, were prepared in scallop shells. Dishes for scalloped oyster preparation were often shaped like scallop shells. Ornamental dishes unable to withstand the necessary baking temperature are still sometimes made in the shape of scallop shells.

Scallop plate   A plate with scalloped edges.

Scantling   An odd-shaped piece of lumber used in building construction.

Scheele's green   An insecticide similar in nature to Paris green.

Scooter plow A specialized form of **Shovel plow** used for cotton CULTIVATION.

Scour When the soil being plowed does not stick to the PLOW SHOVEL or MOLDBOARD, but rather slides off smoothly.

Scours An alternate name for dysentery in farm animals.

Scraper See **Slip**, **Tongued scraper** or **Hog scraper**.

Scrapple Similar to **Headcheese**, except that cornmeal was mixed with the meat. After cooling, the scrapple was usually cut into thin sections and fried.

Scratcher A one-horse CULTIVATOR that used a series of spring teeth instead of PLOW SHOVELS.

Screw Jack See **Jack screw**.

Screw wrench An alternate name for **Monkey wrench**.

Scruple A unit of weight. There are three scruples to a dram and eight drams to an ounce.

Scythe An implement for cutting grass by hand. It consists (according to current dictionaries) of a curved blade and a long handle. However, early twentieth century mail order catalogues refer to the blade *alone* as a scythe. The scythe was developed and used before the advent of the reaper and MOWING MACHINE for harvesting small grain and cutting grass for hay. During the Depression of the 1930s, it was used by small farmers who could not afford anything else. Also, see **Cradle scythe**.

Scythe snath   Handle for a scythe. Some were straight, but usually they were curved to make handling easier. Snaths were of wood, about two inches in diameter and about five feet long.

Sea island cotton   A very long staple cotton originally grown on islands off the coast of South Carolina and Georgia. It is now mostly grown in the Caribbean.

Second $\frac{1}{12}$ of a prime, i.e., one square inch.

Section   (1) A measure of land. See the appendix for details. Look also in the appendix for HALF SECTION and QUARTER SECTION. (2) See HARROW for a discussion of a harrow section.

Seedbox seeder   The seedbox seeder had a seedbox the length of the swath to be planted. A rotating agitator fed the seed out in small continuous streams evenly spaced along the length of the box. By the time the seed hit the ground, the streams had broadened so that reasonably uniform coverage was obtained.

Seeder   Same as planter.

Sen Sen   A breath freshener that was much favored by teenagers to remove the odor of alcohol or tobacco before facing their schoolteachers or parents. It is not clear how much this helped, since the distinctive Sen Sen odor was usually inter-preted as a sign of wrong-doing.

Separator (1) A machine used to separate grain from its straw during threshing. Separators were made as stand-alone machines, but also were an integral part of threshing machines. (2) A machine to separate cream from milk, see **Cream separator**.

Seven-horse combination A seven-horse evener comprised of a **Tripletree** attached to a **Four-abreast evener**.

Sewing chair See **Lady's rocking chair**.

Shafts To steer vehicles or implements pulled by two horses, a tongue attached to the front axle was used, but when there was only one horse, a pair of shafts (light poles) were used instead of a tongue. The shafts were positioned so that they ran along either side of the horse and were attached to the horse's harness by leather straps.

Shay Colloquial for **Chaise**.

Sheep sorrel Wood sorrel (one variety of oxalis). Sometimes chewed for its taste or in salads.

Sheepshire Another name for **Sheep sorrel**.

Sheepskin coat A heavy work coat with a brown duck cloth (cotton) outside and a sheepskin lining.

Shell plate   See **Scallop plate**.

Shield   See **Fender**.

Shipping can   See **Railroad milk can**.

Shock   A number of bundles or arm-
loads of stalks of grain such as wheat, oats,
corn, or sorghum, set together vertically
with the cut ends down. Such an arrange-
ment allowed the stalks to dry and cure and kept the leaves
pointed down to shed rain. Also, the act of making a shock.

Shoe bolt   A special bolt, with a conical head much like that
of a PLOW BOLT, used to attach sled runner shoes to the
runners.

Shoe buttonhook   See **Buttonhook**.

Shoe buttons   Small buttons used on women's
high-topped shoes instead of shoelaces.

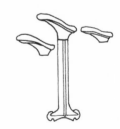

Shoe last   A foot-shaped piece of iron that could be mounted
upside down on a pedestal (last stand) about two feet high. A
shoe placed on the "foot" was held in the right position for a sole
to be nailed to the shoe. When the nails hit the
metal last they were turned back toward the
sole and thus were clinched. (Shoe nails were
specially designed, and often called "clinch"
nails.) Also, see **Shoe peg**. Since only the
front half of a shoe sole usually wore out, only

a half-sole was added. Such half-soles were usually of leather, but during the Depression days of the 1930s, soles were often cut from the tread of worn-out automobile tires. Such soles wore well and were a lot less expensive than leather.

Shoe lift   Shoehorn.

Shoe nail   See **Shoe last** discussion.

Shoe peg   A small hardwood peg used to attach shoe soles to the rest of the shoe. Before attempting to drive the pegs into the leather, holes were made in the leather with a **Peg awl**. While metal shoe nails were sold by the ounce or pound, shoe pegs were usually sold by volume, e.g., by the quart.

Shovel   See PLOW SHOVEL.

Shoveling board   A platform extending out from the back of a wagon box that someone could stand on when beginning to empty the box with a shovel. When the back endgate was removed, even if the wagon box was originally full of something like ear corn, the shovel could be easily filled by sliding along the board.

Shovel plow   A nonwheeled plow intended for CULTIVATION and using one or more shovels instead of a MOLDBOARD.

Shovel point   See PLOW SHOVEL.

Sideboard   A piece of dining room furniture used for storing things such as plates and silverware.

Sideboards   Vertical extensions to the sides of a wagon box that were added when needed to increase the capacity of the wagon box.

Sidebones   A disease of the lateral cartilages of a horse's foot. It was particularly common in draft horses.

Sidesaddle   A saddle especially designed for woman so that they could ride a horse while keeping both legs on the same side of the horse. Such saddles were widely used in the early twentieth century. They were reported to not be nearly as comfortable as regular saddles, but it was not usually considered decorous for a woman to ride a regular saddle.

Sidewinder   (1)A dirty, crooked scoundrel. (2) A variety of small rattlesnake sometimes known as a horned rattlesnake. See SIDEWINDER in the appendix for more details.

Sifter   See **Flour sifter**.

Single-foot plow   A colloquial name for a single-shovel plow.

Singletree   A beam of wood, about three feet long with hooks on each end to which harness tugs or traces were attached. The  middle of the singletree was attached to either an **Evener** or a one-horse implement.

Singletree center clip   The hardware that goes around the center of a singletree and has a ring on it for attaching to a doubletree or a one-horse implement.

Singletree hook and ferrule   A ferrule with an attached hook. The ferrule fitted over the end of a singletree. The hook was for attaching the singletree to a leather tug or steel trace chain.

Skein   The iron (or steel) conical-shaped part that fits over the end of the wooden wagon axle and acts as a bearing for the wheel.

Skeleton plow   Same as **Rod plow**.

Skippers   Larvae of the skipper fly.

Slat moldboard   A MOLDBOARD that, instead of being solid, had wide horizontal slots in it.

Sled corn harvester   See **Corn harvester**.

Sled lister   See **Go-devil**.

Sleigh shoe bolt   See **Shoe bolt**.

Slicker rod weeder   See **Rod weeder**.

Slip   A slip (also sometimes called a scoop, scraper, or road scraper) was the common implement for moving dirt when doing such things as digging ponds or

making fills where large volumes of dirt were needed. Slips came in several sizes, but would normally scoop up about a quarter of a cubic yard of dirt at a time, and were pulled by two horses. The one shown above is in the dumped position.

Slop Despite the word's bad connotation by the twenty-first century, in the early twentieth century it generally meant a soupy hog feed that might contain anything from a milk and ground wheat mixture to kitchen scraps.

Slop basin See **Slop bowl**.

Slop bowl A table dish used to collect inedible parts of the meal. It is not clear that slop bowls were ever very popular.

Slop jar A regional term sometimes used for **Chamber pot**.

Slop pail A bucket used to collect kitchen scraps that were later fed to the hogs.

Small-grain binder See **Grain binder**.

Smith See **Blacksmith**.

Smokehouse A small building designed to be filled with wood smoke and to hold meat to be "smoked." Since smoking could take several days, the operation was only done when the temperature was low enough for the meat to not spoil. To keep the stove producing the smoke from heating up the smokehouse, it was sometimes placed outside the house and the smoke piped in. More often though, a small fire was built on the smokehouse floor (dirt or rock) and tended by the farm children.

Snaffle   A **Bridle bit** made of two joined segments. This was the design most used for workhorse bits.

Snath   See **Scythe snath**.

Sociable   An informal social event such as a **Pie supper**.

Sod cutting plow   See **Rod plow**.

Soja bean   Soybean.

Soldering copper   In the early part of the twentieth century, the same as **Soldering iron**.

Soldering iron   In the early part of the twentieth century, soldering irons were solid copper blocks three or so  inches long with cross sections of about a square inch and having an iron rod extending out from it about eight inches. The rod was pointed so that a wooden handle could be driven onto it. The soldering iron was heated by putting it in a fire. It was taken out of the fire for soldering, and as soon as it cooled to the point that solder could no longer be melted, it had to be reheated.

Sole leather   Leather of the right thickness and quality for making shoe soles.

Songbow   A bow made from a wood stick a few feet long and used as a one-string musical instrument.

Sorghum   The syrup made from boiling down sweet sorghum cane juice (i.e. the syrup also known as **Molasses**).

Sorghum mill   See **Cane juice rollers**.

Sorghum molasses   See **Sorghum** or **Molasses**.

Sorghum syrup   See **Sorghum** or **Molasses**.

Sorgo   Those plants of the genus *sorghum* that were also called sweet sorghums.

Sorgo-syrup   Syrup made of juice from the stalks of various varieties of sorgo. In most rural areas, the syrup was referred to as molasses. Also, see **Molasses**.

Souse   A meat mixture similar to headcheese but not specifically using meat from a hog's head. (See also **Headcheese**.)

Sow belly   The cut of pork that, when cured, became bacon. Late twentieth century dictionaries refer to sow belly as bacon.

Spade   Another name for the **Bull tongue**, a CULTIVATOR plow point shaped somewhat like a tongue.

Spark advance   Early automobiles had a spark control that allowed the timing of the spark with respect to the position of the piston to be manually adjusted. Retarded too much, the engine would not run well at high speeds. Advanced too much and the engine would fire too soon and kick while being cranked. This sometimes resulted in a broken arm.

Spear   A term sometimes used instead of **Pole cap**.

Spike-tooth harrow   A HARROW with straight teeth that look much like railroad spikes.

Spittoon   See **Cuspidor**.

Spokeshave   A small drawknife with a blade only about three inches long that was intended to be used in making wagon spokes and other rounded items.

Spoon holder   A porcelain or glass piece of tableware that looked much like a short vase. It was used at the table for holding spoons.

Spoon jar   See **Spoon holder**.

Spooner   See **Spoon holder**.

Spring-tooth harrow   A HARROW with teeth that are flat, curved, pointed bars of spring steel.

Springhouse   A small building built over a spring and arranged so that the cool water from the spring could be used to keep milk and butter cool.

Spuding   Spuding was the name applied to the method of drilling oil wells before the introduction of rotary drilling. Spuding involved the repeated dropping of a long, heavy bit to break-up the soil or rock. Periodically, the bit was pulled out of the hole and a tubular bucket (a much heavier version of the **Well bucket** for a drilled water well) used to haul up the resulting mud.

Stalk cutter   An implement that could be pulled over a field of long stalks, such as those left after corn has been picked or sorghum cane headed, and chop the stalks into short lengths. The shorter lengths could then more easily be turned under by a TURNING PLOW.

Stanley steamer   Probably the most successful and well-known steam-powered automobile made in the U.S. (Newton, MA). The first one was built in 1897 and the last one in 1927.

Star   In the period from 1903 to 1928, there were several companies in the U.S. and at least one in Great Britain that made "Star" automobiles. The most successful was the Star from the Durant Motor Company in Lansing, MI.

Steam road   A term used near the end of the nineteenth century for public conveyances running on a track and using steam power to move the car(s).

Steelie   A marble-size steel ball bearing used as a marble taw. Because of their extra weight, steelies worked better than regular taws, but because they tended to chip, glass marbles were generally not allowed in games.

Steelyard   A weighing scale in which the object to be weighed was suspended near the end of the shorter arm of a straight pivoted beam and a light counterbalancing weight (**Poise**) moved along the longer arm until the beam was balanced. Also, see **Cotton scale**.

Stereoscope   A lightweight handheld optical instrument for viewing side-by-side photographs taken with a special camera so that the combined image appeared to be three-dimensional. The two photographs were printed on a card about the size of a post card.

Stereoscopic slide

Sticky shield   A panel covered with a sticky layer (much like present day flypaper) used to trap insects. Such shields were sometimes made of canvas in the form of a large open-bottomed-and-ended box that was mounted on wheels and dragged (by horse or mule) over a row of plants. One formulation of the sticky layer was paint made by boiling five pounds of rosin in a half gallon of castor oil. It was then applied hot to the canvas.

Stillyard   Colloquial for **Steelyard**.

Sting tongue tree   See **Hercules-Club tree**.

Stitching horse   See **Harness horse**.

Stomp dance   See **Indian stomp dance**.

Stone   One stone = 14 pounds. It is an archaic English unit of weight that was sometimes still used in the U.S. at the beginning of the twentieth century.

Stop-back   A fruit tree injury thought to be caused by the **Tarnished-plant bug**.

Stove bolt   A small bolt with a square nut and a screwdriver-slotted head. While the bolts were intended to hold the sheet metal parts of stove together, they were widely used for general repair work.

Stove lid   Wood- and coal-burning cook stoves had CAST IRON stovetops with several circular openings seven or eight inches in diameter that were covered with removable CAST IRON lids. Cooking utensils were set over the holes and, when a lid was removed, the utensil was directly over the fire. To give some temperature control, at least one lid was generally made up of a graduated nest of two or three concentric, flat CAST IRON rings so that the size of the hole open to the firebox could be adjusted by choosing the number of rings removed.

Stove lid lifter   A removable handle used  to move stove lids.

Stove poker   See **Poker**.

Stove polish   The outside of stoves was generally "painted" black with stove polish but, because of the heat, the coating tended to burn off. To keep the stove from rusting required the regular application of polish. Since the stove would likely still be hot when the new polish was added, the polish was generally waterbased to eliminate any fire hazard.

Stovepipe damper   See **Damper**.

Stover   The mature stalks of grain such as corn and grain sorghum after the grain is removed. Stover was often used for winter livestock feed.

Straight-tooth harrow   Another name for a **Spike-tooth harrow**.

Strop   A thin leather strap about two inches wide and twenty inches long used for burnishing a straight razor edge after the razor had been sharpened on a **Whetstone (Whetrock)**. Razor strops were also sometimes used instead of switches for administering punishment to small boys.

Struck bushel   What is commonly referred to as a "bushel," i.e., four pecks, or 32 quarts.

Studebaker   Originally a wagon manufacturer, but in the 1920s started making automobiles. The last Studebaker built in the U.S. (South Bend, IN) was in 1964.

Please Write
for prices and detailed information.
We will send you literature describing wagons best adapted to your particular business.

Studebaker
KANSAS CITY

There Are More
Studebaker Delivery Wagons in use than all other makes combined.

Quality and Reputation have made this so.

From an ad in the March 11, 1911, *Weekly Implement Trade Journal*

Stump puller   A horse-powered capstan-like device used for pulling stumps out of the ground.

Stutz   The Ideal Motor Car Company of Indianapolis, IN began making the Stutz racing cars in 1911. In 1913, the name was changed to the Stutz Motor Car Company of America, and passenger cars were made until 1935.

Stutz Bearcat   A Stutz Motor Car Company sports car introduced in 1914.

Subsoil plow   A plow that had no MOLDBOARD and was used to plow deeper than a conventional **Turning plow** in order to break up the subsoil.

Sugar sifter   A container somewhat larger than a saltshaker that was intended to dispense sugar in the same manner as a saltshaker dispenses salt.

Sugar tit   A small amount of sugar wrapped in a piece of cloth and used as a baby pacifier.

Sugar tree   Sugar maple tree.

Sulky plow   A horse-drawn one-bottom riding plow.

Sulky rake   A horse-drawn hay rake that had a seat for the operator. This rake preceded, and was replaced by, the side-delivery rake.

Surface cultivator   A CULTIVATOR with blades or shovels not penetrating very deeply into the soil. Also, see **Weeder**.

Surface packer   An implement such as a heavy roller or a CULTIPACKER that could be used to pack the surface of a plowed field.

Surrey   A light, four-wheeled conveyance intended for personal transportation that was much like a **Buggy** except that it had two seats and could accommodate more passengers.

Swage   A die-like tool designed for use by blacksmiths for shaping metal.

Swamp cooler   An evaporative cooler used before the advent of the refrigerated-air room air conditioner. Cooling was done by evaporating water. Swamp coolers only worked well in dry climates.

Sward   Turf. One early writer described it as being formed of thousands of wire-like fibrous roots interwoven in every direction.

Sweat collar   Same as horse **Collar pad**.

Sweep rake   See **Buck rake**.

Sweep stock   A one- or two-horse **Walking plow** that was much like a **Lister**, only more lightly constructed. So called because the PLOW SHOVEL normally used on it was a SWEEP.

Sweetbreads   The thymus gland of young beef, hogs, and sheep. Sweetbreads are now much prized by food lovers, but during Depression days, they were primarily eaten just after an animal was butchered to keep from wasting any edible portion of the carcass.

Swinging bridge (1) colloquially, a short suspension bridge across a creek or small river. Generally, such bridges were built without benefit of engineering help and from whatever appropriate materials could be found locally. (2) An alternative to a drawbridge. In this case, a section of the bridge pivoted on a single pier and could be rotated horizontally to allow boat passage on either side of the pier.

Swingle A flat wood member used to thresh grain. See also **Swipple**.

Swingletree Same as **Singletree**.

Swiple See **Swipple**.

Swipple The part of a **Flail** used to hit the grain being threshed with a flail.

Swivel-tail See first entry under **Wiggle-tail**.

T

Table salt A small bowl, usually glass, designed to hold small quantities of salt. Table salts were intended to be included with each table place setting and replace a saltshaker on the table.

Tailor's goose A heavy iron used by tailors. The name goose came from the curved handle that somewhat resembled the necks of two geese.

Tallow   Rendered fat of cattle and sheep.

Tambour clock   A mantle clock with a wide base that flared into a tambour-like shape that surrounded the top part of the dial. Such clocks were also sometimes referred to only as "tambours."

Tame grass   Cultivated grass, i.e., grass that has been selected and grown in a manner to accentuate specific characteristics.

Tame hay   Hay made from **Tame grass**.

Tame pasture   A pasture, comprised, not of native, but of **Tame grass**.

Tanbark   Chips of tree bark rich in tannin, commonly oak tree bark. As an aside, the leaves of trees like elm have little tannin in them and can be safely eaten by cattle, while oak leaves have so much tannin in them that, while they can be eaten by horses, cannot be safely eaten by cattle. During the Depression of the 1930s and during times of severe drought, it was not uncommon to chop down any available elm trees so cattle could eat the leaves.

Tar camphor   Naphthalene.

Tarnished-plant bug   An insect pest that in the early twentieth century caused substantial **Bush-head** and **Stop-back** fruit tree injuries.

Tatting   A kind of open weave lace-like cloth made by hand, or the act of making it.

Teakettle A covered metal pot with a bail and a spout. Before hot water heaters were available, teakettles were kept on the kitchen stove to supply hot water for such things as shaving and hand washing. A teakettle full of  boiling water was also a convenient place to cook hard-boiled eggs. (When kitchen stoves burned either coal or wood, they usually had a fire in them all day, so a teakettle on the stove provided a daylong source of hot water.)

Tedder A horse-drawn implement for fluffing hay after it was cut, and primarily after windrowing. It was intended to stir up and turn over extra heavy hay to help the part near the ground to dry, or to help the drying of cut grass that had been dampened by an unexpected rain. In general, tedding was done after wilting, but before leaves became dry enough to be brittle and be lost during the remainder of the haying operation. Tedders were used primarily in the more humid parts of the country and were seldom seen in the West, Southwest, and Midwest.

Terracer A horse-drawn bladed implement used to make terraces.

Texas Stock A one- or two- horse walking plow, used for CULTIVATION and for making furrows for a one-row planter (**Corn planter**).

Thills See **Shafts**.

Throw Before the use of squeeze chutes, it was sometimes necessary to "throw" horses and cattle before some veterinary treatments. Throwing consisted of causing the animal to lose its footing and lay on its side on the ground.

Tickle tongue tree   See **Hercules-Club tree**.

Tierce   A unit of liquid volume, 42 gallons (⅓ **Pipe**).

Tin   A common name for galvanized corrugated sheet iron, which was primarily used for roofing. Tin was also the name used for the thin sheet steel used to make tin cans.

Tin lizzy   Slang for early automobiles, usually Ford Model Ts.

Tire   Late in the nineteenth century, "tire" usually meant the iron rim of a wooden wagon wheel. Only later did "tire" begin referring to the hollow cylindrical cross-section rubber outer portion of bicycle and automobile wheels.

Tire bender   A set of heavy rollers used to bend strips of iron into circular wheel rims (usually wagon wheel tires).

Tire rim   Steel rims were fitted inside the tires of early automobiles, and then the rims bolted to the automobile wheels. The illustration shows one variety, described as a split rim. When 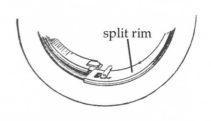 the rim ends were slid apart as shown, the rim could be partially collapsed and easily removed from the inside of the tire.

Tire shrinker   See **Wagon tire shrinker** discussion.

Tire upsetter   See **Wagon tire shrinker** discussion.

Toast water   Made by soaking heavily browned toast in water and then straining.

Tobacco transplanter   See **Transplanter**.

Tongue   A long pole attached to the front wheels of an implement and held between two horses by the horses' harness. As the horses turned, they moved the tongue and changed the direction of travel of the front wheels.

Tongued scraper   A scraper for scooping up dirt. There were also nontongued versions that were usually called **Slips**.

Toothache tree   See **Hercules-Club tree**.

Top strap   The leather strap that held the top of the **Hames** tight around the collar (equivalent to the **Hame strap** at the bottom of the **Hames**).

Tourist court   What, by the middle of the twentieth century, was called a motel. Tourist courts were usually a series of very small one-room buildings separated from each other by the width of an automobile.

Tourist home   What, by the middle of the twentieth century, was called a bed-and-breakfast.

Trace chain   A long-linked chain connecting each harness hame to the **Singletree**. A pair of trace chains transmitted the pull of the horse to the singletree. (See also **Traces**.)

Traces   Either heavy laminated leather straps, or sections of chain, used to connect harness hames to singletrees.

Transplanter   An implement that made a furrow, gave a periodic squirt of water into the furrow, and had seats for two people whose task was to put a plant in each wet spot. Transplanters were commonly used for tobacco and for sweet potatoes.

Tread-power   Treadmill.

Treading   Threshing by walking animals, usually horses, over the heads of grain such as wheat or oats.

Treadle sewing machine   Foot-powered sewing machine.

Treadmill   A machine with an endless belt that an animal can walk on and cause the belt to rotate, thereby converting walking motion into rotary motion. Treadmills, like **Horse powers**, are very old in concept. Roman relief drawings of 100 AD show man-powered machines that look much like those to be found today for mice to play on.

Treenail   See **Trunnel**.

Triple-tree   A three-horse **Evener**.

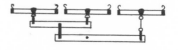

Trunnel   A wooden dowel used to prevent a wooden mortise and tenon joint from slipping apart. Trunnels were usually made of a hardwood such as oak or hickory.

Tug   Instead of a trace chain running the entire distance from the hames to singletree, sometimes a wide, laminated leather strap (tug) was used for most of the distance.

Tumbling rod   Instead of a belt, power was transmitted from **Horse powers** by a drive shaft, which ran close enough to the ground for the horses to step over it each time they came around. Once outside the horses' path, the shaft could either be directly coupled or belted to the machine to be powered.

Tun   A unit of liquid capacity. One definition gives eight 31.5-gallon barrels (252 gallons) per tun.

Tune or tuning bow   See **Songbow**.

Tuning eye   A vacuum tube incorporating a cathode ray-incited fluorescent screen on the front of the tube. The tuning eye was used in the late 1930s and early 1940s to provide a visual indication of when a radio was optimally tuned. The tube was mounted in the radio in such a way that the image (a bright, varying width annular sector of the screen) on the tube could be watched while the tuning knob was turned.

Turn plow   Same as a **Walking turning plow**.

Turning plow   See **Walking turning plow** or TURNING PLOW.

Two-way plow   See **Hillside plow**.

V

Vassanater   A spelling sometimes used for **fascinator**.

Velvet bean   A warm-weather annual legume that apparently originated in India and was transplanted to Florida before 1900. The beans are fed to cows and hogs and, in some parts of the world, are used for human consumption.

Victrola   Originally, a phonograph from the Victor Talking Machine Company, Camden, NJ, but it eventually became more of a generic term for any brand of phonograph. The turntables of phonographs of that era were usually powered by wind-up springs. Also, there was no electronic amplification. The grooves of the record caused the phonograph needle to vibrate and it, in turn, caused a metal diaphragm to which it was attached, to vibrate also. The sound from the vibrating metal disk was acoustically coupled to a large megaphone-like horn mounted in the phonograph cabinet.

Vinegar eel   The nematodes sometimes found in mother of vinegar were often called vinegar eels.

W

Wagon box rod   A rod with a head (usually a ring) on one end, and threads on the other end, used at each end of a wagon box to keep the sideboards from spreading apart.

Wagon box strap   A flat iron strip a foot or so long with a threaded rod portion on one end. Such straps were used to anchor the sides of a wagon box to the box bottom.

Wagon jack   A jack intended for raising a wagon axle two or three inches so that a wheel could be removed or partially pulled off for greasing. When a light farm wagon was empty, greasing was generally done by manually lifting one corner of the wagon, sliding  the wheel partially off the iron skein, and putting grease only on the exposed section. Later, after the wheel was reinstalled and began rotating, the grease would work its way over the whole wheel bearing.

Wagon scale   **Cotton scales** were used for weighing many things, but they couldn't accommodate a wagonload of hay or a wagon carrying a half-dozen hogs. For that purpose, there were scales with a platform large enough for a wagon to be driven onto.

Wagon sling   A latticework of rope and timbers that could be put on the bottom of a hayrack before the hay was loaded. Then, to empty the wagon, a hoist could be hooked to the ends of the sling and the entire load picked up at once and placed in the barn.

Wagon tire shrinker   Sometimes, because of things like the tire stretching or the wood parts shrinking, the iron wagon tire would become loose on the wheel. In particular, in dry weather the wheel might dry out and shrink enough for the tire to come off. The cure was to have a blacksmith shrink the tire, using either a tire shrinker or a tire upsetter to compress a section of the tire and thus shorten the tire circumference.

Wagon tire upsetter   See **Wagon tire shrinker**.

Wagon wheel   Until some years into the twentieth century, the outer rim (wagon tire), and the inner thimble which served as a bushing and turned on the axle were, with the exception of a few rivets and hoops, the only metal in a wagon wheel. Just inside the tire was a segmented ring of wood into which one end of the wooden spokes fitted. Each segment of the ring was called a **Felloe**, **Fellow**, or **Felly**. The other end of the spokes fitted into the hub. The latter was usually made from one carefully seasoned piece of wood bound with iron hoops to keep it from splitting.

Wagon wrench   A WROUGHT IRON wrench used for a dual purpose. One was to loosen or tighten the big nuts on wagon axles that held the wheels in place. The other was for pinning the double-tree to the wagon tongue, with the wrench handle being used as the pin. One advantage of such an arrangement was that the horses were automatically disconnected from the wagon before a wheel was intentionally removed.

Wagon yard   Many times a trip to and from town was too long to be made in one day, and an overnight stay was required. In that case, one would often put up at a wagon yard. The yard was not unlike the present day camp grounds with cars, campers, and people all congregated together.

Walking plow   Same as a **Walking turning plow**.

Walking turning plow   A turning plow having two handles and pulled by a team of horses, mules, or oxen. The plow was held in an upright position by a person walking behind it holding the handles.

Warming closet   See **Warming oven**.

Warming ovens   Enclosures that were built into cook-stoves and slightly heated, either by being close to the main oven or by heat from the stovepipe. Warming ovens were used to keep already-cooked food warm until it could be served.

Wash kettle   A large kettle, usually of cast iron, that was used to heat water for clothes washing. Such kettles were set directly over a fire built outside, and not on a stove.

Wash pan   A pan used for holding water while washing one's hands and face.

Washboard   A wooden frame with horizontal metal ribs running across it that clothes were rubbed against during washing. This method superseded the use of rocks to beat the clothes, and was used until the agitator method of washing was introduced.

Washbowl   See **Wash pan**.

Washtub   A circular sheet metal tub about two feet in diameter that was primarily used for washing clothes. It was also used by children as a bathtub, and for catching and holding rainwater running off the house roof.

Water bucket   A bucket used to hold drinking water. When running water was not available (most rural homes), a bucket containing drinking water was kept available. In summer, it was often hung from a porch rafter.

Water dipper   In households where there was no running water, it was common for everyone to drink directly from the dipper used to dip water from the water bucket. At least some recognized the fact that such a  procedure was unsanitary because, by the 1920s, rural grade school students were getting lessons in how to make a throwaway drinking cup from a sheet of tablet paper. (There were, of course, no drinking fountains in rural schools, only a well or cistern and a bucket of water.)

Water dowsing   See **Water witching**.

Water gallon   277.25 cubic inches. See also the discussion with the **Dry gallon** entry.

Water monkey   Originally, a young boy who carried drinking water to a group of field hands such as a threshing or hay-baling crew. Later, the term also included the man who supplied water to the steam engines powering threshing machines. In that case, the water was transported in a water wagon, which was really just a big tank on wheels. Several hundred gallons of water a day was required per steam engine, and the driver (water monkey) filled the tank from the nearest creek or pond with a hand pump mounted on the wagon.

Water switching　Same as **Water witching**.

Water wagon　A wagon carrying a large tank for holding water. Such wagons were used for hauling water to steam-powered threshing machines, and in small towns, for hauling drinking water to individual homes, where it would be stored in a **Cistern**.

Water witching　The use of a small forked branch of a tree to find underground water, and thus determine water well sites. There is no scientific evidence that water witching actually works.

Watering trough　Western movies almost always showed a watering trough in town for the thirsty horses of cow-boys, but when rural families went to town in a wagon (still being done in some regions of the U.S. into the  1930s), their horses also needed water, and most small towns in agricultural areas had a horse-watering trough. The one shown was retired in the 1940s.

Watkins flavoring　Food flavoring sold by Watkins salesmen, whose routes includes most rural homes, which they visited several times a year.

Weeder   CULTIVATORS that were used to break the soil crust over germinating seeds and to destroy young weeds.

Weevil beater   An implement with rotating vanes that was designed to be pulled between rows of cotton to knock weevils from the plants and into a pan of coal oil being dragged along the ground.

Weevil sweeper   An attachment to CULTIVATORS that was intended to knock weevils from cotton plants as the plants were cultivated.

Weld   When blacksmiths were plying their trade, welding was not by electric arc or acetylene torch. The two pieces of iron were heated in a forge, and then beat on an anvil until they stuck (were welded) together.

Well bucket   A bucket used to draw water from a well. For those with a dug well, such a bucket was usually a plain bucket attached to the end of a rope or chain. In the case of drilled wells, the well casing was only a few inches in diameter and an ordinary bucket was too large. For those wells, a special well bucket (bailer) was used that was a galvanized sheet iron tube four or five inches in diameter and four or five feet long. The top of the cylinder had a bail and the bottom incorporated a check valve so that water could enter but not drain out until the bucket was pulled up and the valve tripped.

Well pulley   Same as **Well wheel**.

Well wheel   The pulley used when drawing (pulling) water from a well.

Welsbach mantle   The kind of mantle used in gasoline and propane lanterns to greatly increase the amount of light from the flame. The mantle was originally used with the natural and artificial gaslights of the early 1900s and, for a while after its introduction, was often called the Welsbach mantle from its inventor, Carl von Welsbach.

Wet cupping   Scarifying the skin before cup application so that blood can be drawn through the skin. See **Cupping**.

Whalebone   Not really bone, but a horn-like material found in the mouth of the baleen whale. In the early part of the twentieth century, whalebone was widely used for stays in women's corsets because it was light, flexible, and rustproof.

Wheelbar   Colloquial for wheelbarrow.

Wheelwright   One who made or repaired wheels (usually wooden wagon wheels). In farming communities, the black-smith usually did the repairing.

Whetrock   Same as **Whetstone**, i.e. an abrasive stone used for sharpening things such as knives and axes.

Whetstone   See **Whetrock**.

Whiffletree   A **Singletree**.

Whip socket   A holder, usually mounted on a buggy dash, to hold a whip.

Whippletree   Same as **Whiffletree**.

White alkali   Alkaline soil caused by too high a concentration of the salts magnesium sulfate, sodium sulfate, and sodium chloride.

White lightning   A term sometimes used when referring to bootleg or home-distilled whiskey.

Whitewash   A thin, white wash composed primarily of lime and water. It was sometimes used instead of the more expensive paint to cover walls and fences.

Wiggle-tail   (1) A term sometimes used for a one-row riding CULTIVATOR with wheels that could be guided by moving the seat. (2) A tadpole. (3) A mosquito larva.

William Deering & Co.   By 1880, a major manufacturer of twine-binding harvesters. They later manufactured other farm implements, including MOWING MACHINES.

Willys   An automobile made at various times between 1908 and 1963 by the Willys-Overland Company of Toledo, OH.

Winchester   While Winchester is a longtime firearms manufacturer, the term Winchester usually specifically meant a 30-30 rifle.

Windcharger   A small windmill driving a
six-volt generator. Wind-chargers were used to
keep radio batteries charged after the development of six-volt
(automobile) battery-powered radios and before the advent of
rural power lines.

Windrow   After mowing and initial drying, grass to be used for
hay was raked into rows (windrows). If **Sweep rakes** were used
to gather the hay from the windrows, they ran along the
windrows and gathered up the hay. Otherwise, men with pitch-
forks picked the hay up from the windrows and pitched it onto
a wagon for transport to a stack or barn. Eventually, hay balers
were developed that ran along the windrow and picked up the
hay, so the sweep rake became obsolete.

Wine gallon   231 cubic inches. See also the discussion with
the **Dry gallon** entry.

Winnow   To clean grain by throwing it, shovelful by shovelful,
against the wind.

Winnowing mill   A **Fanning mill**.

WPA   The WPA, or Works Project Administration, was started
by the U.S. Government in 1935 as a program for economic
relief during the Depression years.

Wringer   See **Clothes wringer**.

X

Xylonite   See **Zylonite**.

Y

Yoke   A wooden bar attached by wooden bows to the necks of a pair of draft animals such as oxen. The yoke could then be connected to the implement to be pulled. Yokes tended to choke horses and mules so, for them, collars and harness were used. Also, see **Neck yoke**.

Z

Zylonite   The second edition of *Webster's New International Dictionary (1959)* says it was the original name for celluloid. The 1940 *Merck Index* indicates that celluloid and zylonite are the same. An early twentieth century dictionary says zylonite (xylonite) is similar to celluloid and is made from pyroxylin. The 1895 Montgomery Ward catalog lists both celluloid and zylonite harness rings, which implies that they were different (although they might be of the same material but from different manufacturers).

Appendix

ANVIL HEEL   The opposite end of an anvil from the ANVIL HORN.

ANVIL HORN   The end of an anvil that comes to a point and is shaped somewhat like a horn.

BARREL   (1) A round vessel made of wood staves or of sheet metal. Barrels had a greater length than diameter and those of wood bulged in the middle. (2) A unit of volume. There are no worldwide standards of size, and the official values may change through time. U.S. wine barrel volume (1920s) was 31 gallons. The beer barrel volume was 31.5 gallons, and the British imperial beer barrel contained 36 gallons. At the end of the twentieth century, a barrel of oil was 42 gallons and a barrel of water was 31.5 gallons. In 1866, a gallon was listed in Sweet's *Ready Reckoner* (U.S.) as containing 277.25 cubic inches. By 1920, a U.S. gallon contained 231 cubic inches and, at the beginning of the twenty-first century, still contained 231 cubic inches.

BIG SUMMER GRAPE   A wild grape. See POST OAK GRAPE.

BITUMINOUS COAL   Soft coal. It has a high sulfur content, is cheaper than hard coal, and was normally used for cooking and heating when coal rather than wood was burned.

BLACK JACK   Common name for black oak.

BOLSTER   Part of a wagon. It was a heavy wood beam just slightly shorter than an axle and one was placed between each axle, and the wagon box. There were two bolsters on a wagon.

The rear bolster was directly over the rear axle and firmly fixed to it. The front axle had a wooden beam (sand board) bolted to the top of it. Above that was the front bolster, which was attached to the sand board and front axle with a single loose-fitting king pin. The single pin allowed the front axle to swivel (turn) under the bolster so that the wagon direction could be controlled by the front axle. The looseness, in principle, allowed the front axle to rock from side to side a small amount without affecting the way the box rode on the **Running gear**. Bolsters were usually made of oak or hickory, were about four feet long, and about 4 × 5 inches in cross section.

CAST IRON   An alloy of carbon and iron containing over 1.7 percent carbon. However, carbon contents exceeding about six percent are too weak and brittle to be of much use. Cast iron has a low tensile strength and is quite brittle, but can be cheaply produced in intricate shapes. It was widely used in making such things as MOWING MACHINE frames, heavy lugged wheels, and large gears with teeth not subjected to high stress. Because of its brittleness and hardness, little machining was done on cast iron parts.

CHILLED IRON   CAST IRON that is rapidly cooled to make it harder and more wear resistant.

CLYDESDALE   A large workhorse that was developed in Scotland, probably from heavy black and dun stocks being imported into Great Britain by the eleventh century.

COMBINE   An implement that first cuts off grain stalks, and then strips the grain from the stalk. The combine replaced the grain binder and the threshing machine combination. Early combines were the leviathans of the horse-powered world. Near the beginning of the twentieth century they were so large that up to forty horses were required to pull them, and the driver sat nearly twenty feet in the air.

COVERED BRIDGE   A bridge with wooden trusses and a roof so that the trusses were protected from the weather.

CULTIPACKER   They consisted of a series of iron wheels, each only a few inches wide, strung together side by side and were used to break up dirt clods in plowed fields.

CULTIVATING PLOW   See CULTIVATOR.

CULTIVATION   Cultivation is the plowing done after crops come up in order to control the weeds. For weeding, hand tools such as hoes were used for centuries before equipment suitable for being pulled by draft animals was developed. In fact, the term "hoe" was so ingrained that when first introduced, English cultivating plows, and some American ones as well, were called horse hoes. Unlike turning plows, which turn over a ribbon of soil, grass, and weeds, cultivation plows are aimed more at stirring and scratching the top soil.

CULTIVATOR   A plow intended to be used for CULTIVATION.

CUTTER BAR   The part of a MOWING MACHINE that holds and guides the knife. It is also sometimes called a SICKLE BAR.

DEEP WELL PUMP   A pump designed for pumping water from wells with water levels more than about 25 feet below the pump location. Such pumps are designed so that the pump cylinder is near the well water level and the water is forced to the surface rather than being sucked to it.

DISC   Same as DISK.

DISK   (1) A round thin steel plate, usually dished, that is sometimes used instead of a PLOW SHOVEL or MOLDBOARD. (2) To cultivate or HARROW with an implement that uses disks instead of teeth or shovels.

DISK HARROW   The basic design used a series of slightly cupped metal disks mounted a few inches from each other on a common axle. Until the end of the horse-drawn disk, axle bearings were made of an oil-soaked tough wood such as maple. Without precision dust seals, such bearings lasted much better in harsh and gritty work conditions than the metallic varieties.

DISK PLOW   A TURNING PLOW that uses heavy DISKS about 20 or 24 inches in diameter instead of a conventional MOLDBOARD.

DRAWING   When blacksmithing, the stretching of a piece of iron to reduce its thickness.

DRILL   See GRAIN DRILL.

FOX GRAPE   *Vitus labrusca.* A wild grape particularly attractive to foxes, raccoons, skunks, and opossums. Also known as Northern muscadine, and as swamp grape.

FROG   (1) Part of a turning plow that helps hold the landside and moldboard together. (2) The central part of a horse's hoof.

FROST GRAPE   A wild grape. See POSSUM GRAPE.

GARDEN PLOW   A small, light-framed plow with a wheel on the front of the frame. This plow is designed to be pushed by hand and is used in gardening.

GIN   Generally a cotton gin, which is a collection of machines to separate cotton fibers from cottonseed and then bale the fibers.

GRAIN DRILL   An implement for planting small-grain seed. Several streams of seed are dropped down separate tubes into narrow individual furrows made by small shovels or discs just ahead of the seed tubes. The name "drill" originated from these streams of seed and an old meaning of the word drill, which was "to trickle or dribble." Drill sizes varied from one-horse models through the two-horse size up to four- and six-horse models that could plant about 12 feet at a time. The drill dates back in crude form to at least 1600 A.D. and was introduced into the U.S. from England around 1840.

GUARD   Part of a mowing machine SICKLE BAR.

GUINEA   A fowl somewhat smaller than a chicken that was sometimes raised, along with chickens, to be eaten. Guinea eggs are smaller than those of chickens, and guineas are wilder than chickens.

HALF SECTION   A rectangular block of land measuring ½ mile by one mile, and containing 320 acres. Unless just being used to indicate 320 acres, a "half section" was understood to be one-half of a section.

HARDIE   Variant of HARDY.

HARDY   A heavy chisel designed to fit upright in the HARDY-HOLE of an anvil.

HARDY-HOLE   A hole about one inch square in the heel of an anvil for holding the square shank of such tools as HARDIES and **Swages**.

HARROW   Harrows are the primary implements used to break up dirt clods, fill in holes, and generally level the ground after it has been broken by a turning plow. One of the earlier approaches to harrowing, and one that survived on a limited scale through many centuries, was merely to drag a tree limb with plenty of branches on it over the ground. Harrows to be pulled by horses were made in five-foot wide sections, with provisions for linking them together side-by-side to make them wider. Each section was considered a load for one horse. Thus, if three sections were linked together side-by-side, three horses were used to pull the combination.

HEEL   See ANVIL HEEL.

MARE   Female horse.

MOLDBOARD   The moldboard is the curved part of a turning plow that turns over and pulverizes the slice of earth cut by the PLOWSHARE.

MOWER KNIFE   See discussion in MOWING MACHINE entry.

MOWING MACHINE   A machine for cutting grass or weeds, primarily grass used for hay, but also to cut and control weeds. Mowing machines are an American invention, with the first patent being issued in 1812. By 1850, the machine was reasonably well developed. After 1900, roller bearings and rubber (automobile type) tires were about the only additions made. Horse-drawn mowing machines were pulled by two horses and would usually cut a swath of five feet, although both narrower and wider machines were available. Actual cutting was done by the MOWER KNIFE, a long bar with a row of perhaps twenty triangular sections, each about three inches long, riveted to it. The knife moved back and forth saw-fashion along a track in the SICKLE BAR. Power was transmitted from heavy, lugged wheels through gears, a crank, and a pitman rod (connecting rod) to the SICKLE BAR. By the beginning of the twenty-first century, the reciprocating sickle bar was being phased out in favor of rotating blades.

MOWING MACHINE KNIFE   See discussion of MOWER KNIFE in MOWING MACHINE entry.

MULE   The mule is a cross between a male donkey (jack) and a MARE. Because of the large difference between the donkey and horse families, the offsprings (mules) ordinarily do not reproduce and are thus not considered as a separate breed.

Mules have short, thick heads, long ears, thin legs, small hoofs, and little hair on the root of the tail. They are most famous for their great stubbornness, loud braying or "heehawing," and bad disposition. Mules were never as common as horses in the U.S. and, in the peak horse year of 1918, there were 21 million horses, and only about five million mules.

NAKED CUTTER BAR   A mowing machine CUTTER BAR without GUARDS.

PERCHERON   A large draft horse that originated in the La Perche region of Southwestern France. It resulted from the crossing of large horses from Norway or Eastern Europe with the Oriental horses of the Turks, Barbs, and Arabs.

PLANTER   A farm implement designed to plant crop seed. There are several distinctly different avenues available for planting the many different sizes and shapes of seeds, but each of them consists of the same two basic operations. The first places the seeds in the desired location. The second properly covers them so that they are both protected from birds and kept moist enough to germinate. For the latter, there is a minimum depth of covering necessary. Depending on the crop and soil, this minimum depth varies but is on the order of an inch. There is also some maximum depth that can be used; otherwise, the fledgling plant will never be able to get to the surface.

PLOW BOLT   A bolt that has a conical head with a flat top and a smaller square shank below the head to keep the bolt from turning as its nut is tightened. Such bolts are used to hold parts of the plow together that have scouring surfaces. The bolt head fits into a conical hole sized so that the top of the head is flush with the **Scouring** surface. If a bolt with a conventional head were used, the head would prevent good scouring and would eventually wear away.

PLOW BOTTOM   The base of a turning plow, which is composed of those parts that lift, turn, and invert the soil.

PLOW SHOVEL   A detachable pointed piece of flat metal attached to the frame of a plow and used not to turn over the soil (i.e., a TURNING PLOW) but to break-up and stir it. There were/are many shapes of such points. See also **Bull tongue**, **Calf tongue**, and SWEEP.

PLOWSHARE   The part of a TURNING PLOW that provides the cutting edge. It incurs most of the wear and must be periodically sharpened and, less often, replaced.

POSSUM GRAPE   A wild grape about the size of a pea that is mostly skin and seeds. Possum grape is a colloquial name applied to at least two different varieties of grapes, *Vitus virginiana* and *Vitus vulpina*. The latter was also called winter grape, sour winter grape, frost grape, and fox grape.

POST OAK GRAPE   A wild grape (*Vitis Lincecumii*) often found climbing post oak trees.

PRICKLY ASH   Also see **Hercules-Club tree** in the main text. Another species, more like a shrub, is also called prickly ash. This species has pinnate leaves, and flowers and berries in small clusters along the sides of the branches instead of in large clusters at the end of the branches.

PRITCHEL HOLE   A hole about three-eighths inch in diameter in the end of an anvil opposite the horn. The end of a punch can go into the hole after punching through a piece of metal.

QUARTER SECTION   A square block of land of ½ mile along each side, containing 160 acres and, unless being used only as a unit of area measurement, located so that it was one of four equal-size portions of a section.

RIVERBANK GRAPE   Same as RIVERSIDE GRAPE.

RIVERSIDE GRAPE   *Vitus vulpina,* a wild grape found in the Eastern US along creeks and rivers. See POSSUM GRAPE.

SAND GRAPE   A wild grape. See POST OAK GRAPE.

SECTION   A mile-square piece of land. It contains 640 acres.

SECTION LINE   The imaginary line forming the boundary along one side of a land SECTION.   County roads are often routed along section lines.

SHARE   See PLOWSHARE.

SHIRE   A large workhorse developed in England, presumably from black and dun stocks that were being imported into Great Britain by the eleventh century.

SHOVEL POINT   See PLOW SHOVEL.

SICKLE BAR   See CUTTER BAR.

SIDEWINDER   A variety of small rattlesnake sometimes known as a horned rattlesnake. Above each eye is a "horn" which is really an extension of the upper eye shield. The name sidewinder comes from its mode of locomotion, which is unique, not only among rattlesnakes, but among all other North American snakes. Sidewinders can travel in the normal manner of all snakes, but when in a hurry, form their bodies into a series of loops, and throw them forward. This approach facilitates its movement over sand and also causes its motion to be oblique to the direction in which its head points and leads to the name sidewinder. As might be imagined, the sidewinder is found only in the dry desert-like Western States. Its method of moving in sand is not, however, unique to the United States. Similar moving snakes are found in Africa and in some of the Arab nations.

SOFT WATER   Either pure water or water containing salts that do not react with soap to form insoluble soap scum. Before the use of water-softening chemicals, the primary source of soft water was from rain, and rainwater was often caught and saved in washtubs or barrels.

SOUR WINTER GRAPE   A wild grape. See POSSUM GRAPE.

SUFFOLK   A large workhorse developed in England, presumably from black and dun stocks that were being imported into Great Britain by the eleventh century.

SWAMP GRAPE   A wild grape. See FOX GRAPE.

SWEEP   A particular PLOW SHOVEL design. The sweep widths range from about four inches to more than twelve inches.

SWEET POTATO SLIP   A young sweet potato plant of the size usually used for transplanting.

TANK   A term sometimes applied to a pond used to collect and hold water for livestock.

TURKEY GRAPE   See POST OAK GRAPE.

TURNING PLOW   A plow designed to pulverize a ribbon of earth a few inches wide, and turn it over so that surface trash is buried. The turning plow uses a MOLDBOARD to do the turning. The moldboard concept was apparently developed in the eleventh century in the temperate region of Europe. By 1200 A.D., European moldboard plows had developed into ponderous wheeled machines drawn by several oxen, and did more stirring than turning. It took until the mid-1700s for moldboards to advance to the point that they would really turn the soil. Even then, there was no standardization of design, nor any real understanding of the principles involved. That came in the 1780s when Thomas Jefferson in the U.S. and James Small in Scotland began mathematical studies of the moldboard shape that eventually led to rather efficient designs.

WINTER GRAPE   A wild grape. See POSSUM GRAPE.

WROUGHT IRON   An alloy of carbon and iron containing up to 1.2 percent carbon. The iron also contains fine fibers of slag (mostly ferrous silicate) which run in the direction in which the iron ingot is rolled. Wrought iron has high corrosion resistance, is easily welded, and in general is easily worked. It is this variety of iron that is most encountered in the "iron" parts of horse-drawn farm implements.

Acknowledgments

While a large percentage of the words listed here are from my own remembrances, many of my more than 70 acquaintances were unmercifully quizzed about the items and words they used when growing up. They thus deserve, and have, my heartfelt thanks. Kenneth Bean, John Jeter, Symon Post, and Wayne Scott have been particularly helpful. My wife, Delma Runyan, did most of the line illustrations and helped with the proofing.

Bibliography

Agricultural Faculty, Oklahoma A&M College, *Agriculture for Elementary Schools*, American Book Co., NY, 1938.

Ajilvsgi, Geyata, *Wildflowers of Texas*, Shearer Publishing, Bryan, TX, 1984.

Anon, *Common Weeds of the United States*, Dover Publications, Inc., New York, NY, 1971 (originally published by the USDA in 1970).

Anon, *Dyke's Automobile and Gasoline Engine Encyclopedia*, A. L. Dyke, Publisher, St Louis, MO, 1918.

Anon, *Montgomery Ward & Co. Catalog, 1895, 1944.*

Anon, *Sears, Roebuck & Co. Catalog, 1897, 1902, 1908, 1944.*

Anon, *The Merck Index*, fifth edition, Merck & Co. Inc., Rahway, NJ, 1940.

Anon, *The Oxford English Dictionary*, Clarendon Press, Oxford, England, second edition, 1989.

Ardrey, R. L., *American Agriculture Implements*, Arno Press, New York, NY, 1972 (a reprint of an 1894 edition).

Burlingame, Roger, *Henry Ford*, Alfred A. Knopf, New York, NY, 1969.

Chadwick, John, and W. N. Mann (translators), *The Medical Works of Hippocrates*, Blackwell Scientific Publications, Oxford, England, 1950.

Ditmars, Raymond L., *A Field Book of North American Snakes*, Doubleday & Company, Inc. Garden City, New York, NY, 1949.

Georgano, G. N., (editor), *The Complete Encyclopedia of Motorcars, 1885 to the Present*, E. P. Dutton and Company Inc., New York, NY, second edition, 1973.

Hopkins, Albert A. (editor), *The Scientific American Cyclopedia of Formulas*, Scientific American Publishing Co., New York, NY, 1928.

House, Homer D., *Wild Flowers*, The Macmillan Company, New York, NY, 1934. First published in 1918, reissued with new plates in 1961.

Lyman, Henry M., Fenger, Christian, Jones, H. Webster, and W. T. Belfield, *20th Century Family Physician*, Stanton and Van Vliet, Chicago, IL, 1924.

MacGarald, Willis (editor), *Practical Farming and Gardening*, Rand, McNally & Co., Chicago, IL, 1902.

Mandel, Leon, *American Cars*, Stewart, Tabori & Chang, New York, NY, 1982.

Moore, Dwight D., *Trees of Arkansas*, Arkansas Forestry Commission, 1960.

Munson, T.V. *Foundations of American Grape Culture*, T.V. Munson & Son, Denison, TX, 1909.

Neilson, William A., Knott, Thomas A., and Carhart, Paul W. (editors), *Webster's New International Dictionary*, G & C Merriam Company, Springfield, MA 1961.

Periam, Jonathan, *The Home and Farm Manual*, 1884 edition, reprinted by Greenwich House, 1984, distributed by Crown Publishers, Inc., One Park Avenue, New York, NY 10016.

Quarles, Gilford G., *Elementary Photography*, McGraw-Hill Book Company, New York, NY, 1940.

Reich, Herbert J., *Theory and Applications of Electron Tubes*, McGraw-Hill Book Company, New York, NY, 1944.

Rogin, Leo, *The Introduction of Farm Machinery in its Relation to the Productivity of Labor in the Agriculture of the United States during the Nineteenth Century*, Johnson Reprint Corporation, New York, NY, 1966. (Originally by University of California Press, Berkley, CA, 1931.)

Runyan, W. R., *Identifying Horse-Drawn Farm Implements*, iUniverse.com, Lincoln, NE, 2000.

Russell, Thomas H. et al (editors), *Webster's Imperial Dictionary*, The Saalfield Publishing Co., Chicago, IL, 1917.

Seymour, John, *The Forgotten Arts and Crafts*, Dorling Kindersley Publishing, Inc., New York, NY, 2001.

Singer, Charles et al, (editors), *A History of Technology*, Vols 1, 2, 3, 4, Oxford Press, London, England, 1954, 1956, 1957, 1958.

Smith, Alpheus W., *The Elements of Physics*, McGraw-Hill Book Co., Inc., New York, NY, 1938.

Smith, Harris P. *Farm Machinery and Equipment*, McGraw-Hill Book Company, Inc., New York, NY, 1929.

Sweet, I. D. J., *Ready Reckoner*, Robert M. DeWitt, 1868.

Thwing, Leroy, *Flickering Flames*, Charles E. Tuttle Company, Rutland, VT, 1958.

Wigginton, Eliot (editor), *The Foxfire Book*, Anchor Books, Garden City, NY, 1969.

Wigginton, Eliot (editor), *Foxfire 4*, Anchor Press/ Doubleday, Garden City, NY, 1977.

Wigginton, Eliot and Margie Bennett (editors), *Foxfire 9*, Anchor Press/Doubleday, Garden City, NY, 1986.

Wills, Mary Motz and Howard S. Irwin, *Roadside Flowers of Texas*, University of Texas Press, Austin, TX, 1961.